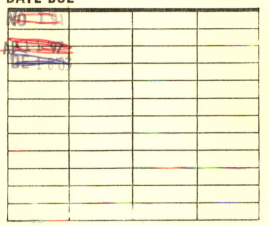

# JAVA
## FACTS AND FANCIES

# JAVA
## FACTS AND FANCIES

BY
AUGUSTA DE WIT

*WITH 160 ILLUSTRATIONS*

SINGAPORE
OXFORD UNIVERSITY PRESS
OXFORD  NEW YORK

Oxford University Press

Oxford   New York   Toronto
Petaling Jaya   Singapore   Hong Kong   Tokyo
Delhi   Bombay   Calcutta   Madras   Karachi
Nairobi   Dar es Salaam   Cape Town
Melbourne   Auckland

and associates in
Beirut   Berlin   Ibadan   Nicosia

OXFORD is a trademark of Oxford University Press

First published by W. P. van Stockum, The Hague, 1912
First issued in Oxford in Asia Paperbacks 1984
Second impression 1985
Reissued as an Oxford University Press paperback 1987
ISBN 0 19 582609 4

Printed in Malaysia by Peter Chong Printers Sdn. Bhd.
Published by Oxford University Press Pte. Ltd.,
Unit 221, Ubi Avenue 4, Singapore 1440

WHEN the Lady Dolly van der
Decken, in answer to questions about
her legendary husband's whereabouts,
murmured something vague about
"Java, Japan, or Jupiter," she had
Java in her mind as the most "impossible" of those impossible places.
And indeed, every schoolboy points
the finger of unceremonious acquaintance at Jupiter; and Japan lies trans-
parent on the egg-shell porcelain of many an elegant tea-table.
But Java? What far forlorn shore may it be that owns the strange-
sounding name; and in what sailless seas may this other Ultima
Thule be fancied to float? Time was when I never saw a globe—
all spun about with the net of parallels and degrees, as with some
vast spider's web without a little shock of surprise at finding
"Java" hanging in the meshes. How could there be latitude and
longitude to such a thing of dreams and fancies? An attempt at

determining the acreage of the rainbow, or the geological strata of a Fata Morgana, would hardly have seemed less absurd. I would have none of such vain exactitude, but still chose to think of Java as situate in the same region as the Island of Avalon; the Land of the Lotos Eaters, palm-shaded Bohemia by the sea, and the Forest of Broceliand, Merlin's melodious grave. And it seemed to me that the very seas which girt those magic shores still keeping their golden sands undefiled from the gross clay of the outer world — must be unlike all other water – tranquil ever, crystalline, with a seven-tinted glow of strange sea-flowers, and the flashing of jewel-like fishes gleaming from unsounded deeps. And higher than elsewhere, surely, the skies, blessed with the sign of the Southern Cross must rise above the woods where the birds of paradise nestle.

Where is it now, the glory and the dream? The soil of Java is hot under my feet. I know—to my cost—that, if the surrounding seas be different from any other body of water, they are chiefly so in being more subject to tempest, turmoil and sudden squalls. I find the benign influences of the Southern Cross—nat a very brilliant constellation by the way—utterly undone by the fiery fury of the noonday-sun; and have learnt to appreciate the fine irony of the inherited style and title as compared with the present habitat, of the said Birds of Paradise. And yet—all disappointing experience notwithstanding, and in spite of the deadly dullness of so many days, the fever of so many sultry nights and the homesickness of all hours— I have still some of the old love for this country left; and I begin to understand something of the fascination by which it holds the Northerner who has breathed its odour-laden air for to long a time; so that, forgetting his home his friends and his kindred in the gray North, he is content to live on dreamely by some lotos-starred lake; and dying, to be buried unter the palm-trees.

AUGUSTA DE WIT.

# FIRST GLIMPSES

A "brownie" of that enchanted garden
that men call Java."

My first impression of Java was not that of effulgent light and overpowering magnificence of colour, generally experienced at the first sight of a tropical country; but, on the contrary, of something unspeakably tender, ethereal and soft. It was in the beginning of the rainy season. Under a sky filmy with diaphanous fleecy texture, in which a tinge of the hidden blue was felt rather than seen, the sea had a pearly sheen, with here and there changefully flickering white lights, and wind-ruffled streaks of a pale violet. The slight haziness in the air somewhat dulled the green of innumerable islets and thickly-wooded reefs, scattered all over the sea; and, blurring their outlines, seemed to lift them until they grew vague and airy as the little clouds of a mackerel sky, wafted hither and thither by the faintest wind. In the distance the block of square white buildings on the landing-place—pointed out as the railway station and the custom houses—stood softly outlined against a background of whitish-grey sky and mist-blurred trees.

Slowly the steamer glided on. And, as we now approached the roadstead of Batavia, there came swimming towards the ship numbers of native boats, darting

out from between the islets, and diving up out of the
shadows along the wooded shore, like so many water-
fowl. Swiftest of all were the "praos", very slight
hulls, almost disappearing under their one immense
whitish-brown sail, shaped like a bird's wing, and
thrown back with just the same impatient fling—ready
for a swoop and rake—so exactly resembling sea-gulls
skimming along, as to render the comparison almost a
description. On they came, drawing purplish furrows
through the pearly greys and whites of the sea. And,
in their wake, darting hither and thither with the jerky
movements of water-spiders, quite a swarm of little
black canoes—hollowed-out tree-trunks, kept in balance
by bamboo outriggers, which spread on either side like
sprawling, scurrying legs. As they approached, we saw
that the boats were piled with many-tinted fruit, above
which the naked bodies of the oarsmen rose, brown
and shiny, and the wet paddle gleamed in its leisurely-
seeming dip and rise, which yet sent the small skift
bounding onward. They were along-side soon, and the
natives clambered on board, laden with fragrant wares.
They did not take the trouble of hawking them about,
agile as they had proved themselves, but calmly squatted
down amid their piled-up baskets of yellow, scarlet,
crimson, and orange fruit—a medley of colours almost
barbaric in its magnificence, notwithstanding the soberer
tints of blackening purple, and cool, reposeful green;
and calmly awaited customers. Under the gaudy ker-
chiefs picturesquely framing the dark brows, their
brown eyes had that look of thoughtful—or is it all
thoughtless?—content, which we of the North know
only in the eyes of babies, crooning in their mother's
lap. And, as they answered our questions, their speech
had something childlike too, with its soft consonants

"Fishing praos, their diminutive hulls almost disappearing under the one tall whitish-brown sail, shaped like a bird's wing and flung back, as if ready for a swoop and rake."

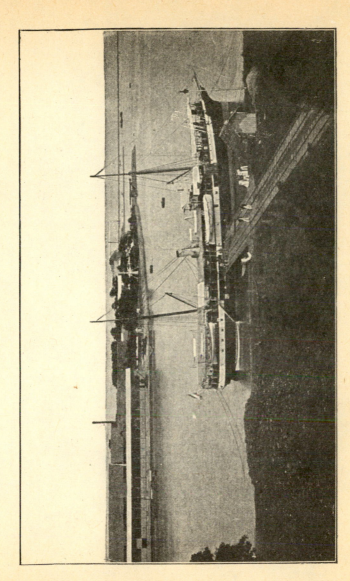

"The ship lay still, and we trod the quay of Tandjong Priok."

and clear vowels, long-drawn-out on a musical modulation, that glided all up and down the gamut. They had a great charm for me, their flatness of features and meagreness of limbs notwithstanding; and I thought, that, if not quite the fairies, they might well be the "brownies" of that enchanted garden that men call Java.

But alas! for day-dreaming—the gruff authoritative voice of the quartermaster was heard on deck; and—after the manner of goblins at the approach of the Philistine—all the little brownies vanished. They were gone in an instant; and, in their pretty stead, came porters, cabin-stewards with trunks, and passengers in very new clothes. For we were fast approaching; and, presently, with a big sigh of relief, the steamer lay still, and we trod the quay of Tandjong Priok.

It would seem as if the first half hour of arrival must be the same everywhere, all the world over; but here, even in the initial scramble for the train, one notices a difference. There is a crowd; and there is no noise. No scuffling and stamping, no cries, no shouting, no gruff-voiced altercations. All but inaudibly the bare-footed coolies trot on, big steamer-trunks on their shoulders; they do not hustle, each patiently awaiting his turn at the office and on the platform; and, as they stand aside for some hurrying, pushing European, their else impassible faces assume a look of almost contemptuous amazement. Why should the "orang blanda" * thus discourteously jostle them? Are there not many hours in a day, and many days to come after this? And do they not know that "Haste cometh of the evil?"

The train has started at last, and is hurrying through a wild, dreary country, half jungle, half marshland. From the rank undergrowth of brushwood and bulrushes

* "People from Holland" the name for Europeans generally.

rise clumps of cocoanut palms, their dark shaggy crowns strangely massive above the meagre stems through which the distant horizon gleams palely. In open spaces young trees stand out here and there, half strangled in the festoons of a purple-blossomed liana that trails its tendrilled length all over the lower shrub-wood. Thickets of bamboo bend and sway in the evening wind.

To the right stretches a long straight canal, dull as lead under the lustreless sky; the breeze, in passing, blackens the motionless water, and a shiver runs through the dense vegetation along the edge—broad-leaved bananas, the spreading fronds of the palmetto, and mimosas of feathery leafage, above which the silver-grey tufts of bulrushes rise. After a while the jungle diminishes and ceases; and a vast reach of marshy country stretches away to the horizon. We neared it as the sun was setting. Though it had not broken through the clouds, the fiery globe had suffused their whiteness with a deep, dull purple as a smouldering flames. A tremulous splendour suddenly shot over the rush-beds and rank waving grasses of the marshy land; the shining reed-pricked sheets of water crimsoned; and along the canal moving like an incandescent lava stream, the broadly curving banana leaves seemed fountains of purple light, and the palmetto and delicate mimosa fronds grew transparent in the all-pervading rosiness—almost immaterial. Even after the burning edge of the sun, perceived for a brief moment, had sunk away, these marvellous colours did not fade; softly shining on, they seemed to be the natural tint of this wonderful land—independent of suns and seasons. Then, all at once, they were extinguished by the rapidly-fallen dusk, as a fire might be under a shower of ashes; and, a few minutes after, it was night.

At the lamplit station of Batavia I hailed one of the vehicles waiting outside—a curious little two-wheeled conveyance, which, with its enormous lanterns, airily supported roof, and long shafts between which a diminutive pony trotted, looked like a fiery-eyed cockchafer that darts about, moving its long antennae. I hoisted myself on to the sloping seat, and, for some time was driven through an avenue, the trees on either side of which made a cloudy darkness against the pale strip of sky overhead. There was an incessant high-pitched twittering of birds among the leaves; and, every now and then, a fragrance of invisible flowers came floating out on the windless air. We passed a tall building, shimmering white through the darkness—the Governor-General's palace I was told. Then the horse's hoofs clattered over a bridge, and, past the turn of the road, a long row of brilliant windows flashed up, with a white blaze of electric light in the distance.

Past the resplendent shop-windows on the left side of the street—the other remaining dark, featureless—a leisurely crowd moved; open carriages, bearing ladies to some evening entertainment, bowled along; a many-windowed club-building blazed out; a canal shone with a hundred slender spears of reflected light—I had reached my destination, the suburb of Rijswijk.

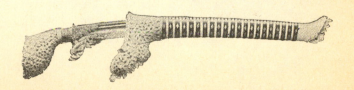

# A BATAVIA HOTEL

If, in this commonplace-loving age, there be one thing more commonplace and utterly devoid of character than another, it is a hotel. Hotels! where are railroads there are they. The locomotive scatters them along its shining path together with cinders, thistleseeds, and tourists. They are everywhere; and everywhere they are the same. The proverbial peas are not so indistinguishably alike. Surely, a whimsical imagination may be pardoned for fancying a difference between the pods "shairpening" in some Scotch kailyard, the petits-pois coquettishly arranged in Chevet's shop-window, and the Zuckererbsen mashed down to a green pulse in some strong-jawed Prussian's plate—a difference, the far and faint and fanciful analogy to the more obvious one between the gudeman, the French chef, and the Königlich Preussischer Douanen-Beamten-Gehilfe who own the said peas. But a hotel, on whatever part of Europe it may open its dull window-eyes, has not even a name native of the country, and declaring its citizenship. The genius of speech despairs of making a difference in the name, where there is none in the thing; and thus, from Orenburg to Valentia, and from Hammerfest to Messina, a hôtel is still called a hotel, and the traveller still expects and finds the same Swiss portier and the same red velvet portières, the same indescribable smell of sherry, stewed-meat, and cigars in the passages, the same funereally-clad waiters round the table d'hôte, and the same dishes upon it. Thus I thought in my old European days. But since, I have come to Java, and I have seen a Batavia hotel—*a rumah makan*. Ah! that was a surprise, a shock, a revelation—I would say "un frisson nouveau" if Batavia and shivering were compatible terms. "Un étouffement nouveau" better expressed my sensations, as it flashed upon me in full noon-day glory. Noon is its own time, its hour of hours, the instant when those opposing elements of Batavia street-life—the native population most conspicuous of a morning, and the European contingent preponderant in the evening—attain that exact equipoise which gives the place its particular character; and when the conditions of sky, air and earth are attuned to truest harmony with it.

The great, strong, full noon-day sun beats on the stuccoed buildings, heating their whiteness to an intolerable incandescence. It has set the garden ablaze, burning up the long grey shadows of early morning to round patches of a charred black, that cling to the foot of the trees; and making the air to quiver visibly above the scorched yellow grass-plots. Among their dark leafage, the hibiscus flowers flare like living flame; and the red-and-orange blossoms, dropping from the branches of the Flame of the Forest, seem to lie on the path like smouldering embers. Through this blaze of light and colour, move groups of gaudily-draped natives—water-carriers, flower-sellers, fruit-vendors, pedlars selling silk and precious stones—their heads protected from the sun by enormous mushroom-shaped hats of plaited straw, and their shining shoulders bending under a bamboo yoke, from the ends of which dangle baskets of merchandise. Small, brown, chubby children, a necklet their one article of wear, are gathering the tiny, yellow-white blossoms that bespangle the grass under the tanjong trees. Grave-faced Arabs stride past. Chinamen trudge along— lean, agile figures—chattering and gesticulating as they go.

"A seller of fruit and vegetables, his baskets dangling from the ends of a bamboo yoke."

But, among the crowd of orientals, no Europeans are seen, save such as rapidly pass in vehicles of every description, from the jolting dos-à-dos onwards—with its diminutive pony almost disappearing between the shafts—to the elegant victoria drawn by a pair of big Australian horses. But, even when driving, the noon-day heat is dangerous to the Westerner; and the European inmates of the hotel are all in the dark cool verandahs, enjoying a dolce far niente enlivened by chaffering with the natives and drinking iced lemonades, the ladies—here is another surprise for the newcomer! —all attired in what seems to be the native dress of sarong and kabaya! A kabaya is a sort of dressing-jacket of profusely-embroidered white batiste, fastened down the front with ornamental pins and little gold chains; and under it is worn the sarong, a gaudily-coloured skirt falling down straight and narrow, with one single deep fold in front, and kept in place by a silk scarf wound several times round the waist, its ends dangling loose. With this costume, little high-heeled slippers are worn on the bare feet; and the hair is done in native style, simply drawn back from the forehead, and twisted into a knot at the back of the head. Altogether, this style of attire is original rather than becoming.

And, if this must be confessed of the ladies' costume, what must be said of the garb some men have the courage to appear in? A kabaya, and—may Mrs. Grundy graciously forgive me for saying it! for how shall I describe the indescribable, save by calling it by its own, by me never-to-be-pronounced name?—A kabaya and trousers of thin sarong-stuff gaily sprinkled with blue and yellow flowers, butterflies, and dragons!

But all this is only an induction into that supreme mystery, celebrated at noon, the rice-table. Here is indeed, "un étouffement nouveau." All things pertaining to it work together for bewilderment. To begin with; it is served up, not in any ordinary dining-room, but in the "back gallery," a place which is a sight in itself, a long and lofty hall, supported on a colonnade, between the white pillars of which glimpses are caught of the brilliantly-flowering shrubs and dark-leaved trees in the

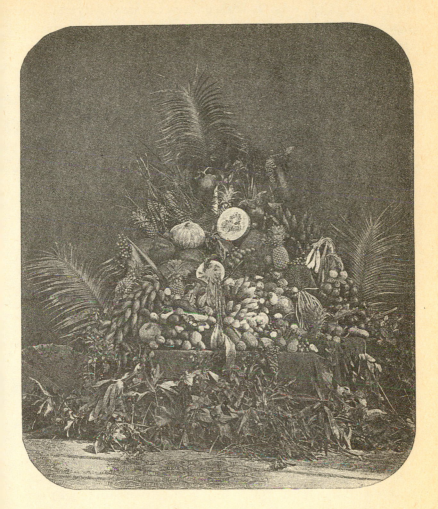

"Pine-apples and mangosteen velvetry rambootan and smooth-skinned dookoo."

garden without. In the second place, it is handed round by native servants, inaudibly moving to and fro upon bare feet, arrayed in clothes of a semi-European cut,

incongruously combined with the Javanese sarong and
head-kerchief. And, last not least, the meal itself is
such as never was tasted on sea or land before. The
principal dish is rice and chicken, which sounds simple
enough. But on this as a basis an entire system of
things inedible has been constructed: besides fish, flesh,
and fricassees, all manner of curries, sauces, pickles,
preserved fruit, salt eggs, fried bananas, "sambals" of
fowl's liver, fish-roe, young palm-shoots, and the gods
of Javanese cookery alone know what more, all strongly
spiced, and sprinkled with cayenne. There is nothing
under the sun but it may be made into a sambal;
and a conscientious cook would count that a lost
day on which he had not sent in at the very least
twenty of such nondescript dishes to the table of
his master, for whose digestion let all gentle souls
pray! And, when to all this I have added that these
many and strange things must be eaten with a spoon
in the right hand and a fork in the left, the reader
will be able to judge how very complicated an affair
the rice-table is, and how easily the uninitiated may
come to grief over it. For myself, I shall never forget
my first experience of the thing. I had just come in
from a ride through the town, and I suppose the glaring
sunlight, the strangely-accoutred crowd, the novel sights
and sounds of the city must have slightly gone to my
head (there are plenty of intoxicants besides "gin"
*vide* the Autocrat of the Breakfast Table). Anyhow, I
entered the "back gallery" with a sort of "here-the-
conquering-hero-comes" feeling; looked at the long
table groaning under its dozens of rice-bowls, scores of
dishes of fowls and fish, and hundreds of sambal-saucers,
arrayed between pyramids of bananas, mangosteens, and
pine-apples, as if I could have eaten it all by way of

"The big kalongs hanging from the topmost branches in a sleep from which the sunset will presently awaken them."

"apéritif;" sat me down; heaped my plate up with everything that came my way; and fell to. What followed I have no words to express. Suffice it to say, that in less time than I now take to relate it, I was reduced to the most abject misery—my lips smarting with the fiery touch of the sambal; my throat the more sorely scorched for the hasty draught of water with which, in my ignorance, I had tried to allay the intolerable heat; and my eyes full of tears, which it was all I could do to prevent from openly gushing down my cheeks, in streams of utter misery. A charitable person advised me to put a little salt on my tongue, (as children are told to do on the tail of the bird they want to catch). I did so; and, after a minute of the most excruciating torture, the agony subsided. I gasped, and found I was still alive. But there and then I vowed to myself I would never so much as look at a rice-table again.

I have broken that vow: I say it proudly. It is but a dull mind which cannot reserve a first opinion, or go back upon a hasty resolve. And now I know *how* to eat rice, I love it. Still, that first meal was a shock. It suddenly brought home to the senses what up to that minute had been noted by the understanding only: the fact of my being in a new country. The glare of the garden without, the Malay sing-song of those dark bare-footed servants, the nondescript clothes of the other guests, united with the tingling and burning in my throat to make me realise the stupendous change that had come over my universe, the antipodal attitude of things in Europe and things in Java. I had the almost bodily sensation of the intervening leagues upon leagues, of the dividing chasm on the unknown side of which I had just landed. And it fairly dizzied me.

Now, the natural reaction following upon a shock of this kind throws one back upon the previous state of things—in the case the ways and manners of the old country—and one stubbornly resolves to adhere to them. But, though this may be natural, it is not wise. I, at least, soon discovered for myself the truth of the old sage's saw: "Verité en decà des Pyrénées, erreur en delà," as applied to the affairs of everyday life; the more so, as oceans and broad continents, the space of thousands of Pyrenean ranges, separate those hither and thither sides, Holland and Java. The home-marked standard of fit and unfit must be laid aside. The soul must doff her close-clinging habits of prejudiced thought. And the wise man must be content to begin life over again, becoming even as a babe and suckling, and opening cherub lips only to drink in the light, the leisure, and the luxuriant beauty of this new country as a rich mother's milk—the blameless food on which to grow up to (colonial) manhood.

But to return to that first "rice-table." After the rice, curries, etc. had been disposed of, beef and salad appeared, and to my infinite astonishment, were disposed of in their turn, to be followed by the dessert—pineapples, mangosteens, velvety "rambootans," and an exceedingly picturesque and prettily-shaped fruit-spheres of a pale gold containing colourless pellucid flesh—which I heard called "dookoo." Then the guests began to leave the table, and I was told it was time for the siesta—another Javanese institution, not a whit less important, it would appear, than the famous rice-table —and vastly more popular with newcomers. Perhaps the preceding meal possesses somniferous virtue; or perhaps, the heat and glare of the morning predispose one to sleep; or, perhaps—after so many years of com-

plaining about "being waked too soon"—the sluggard
in us rejoices at being bidden in the name of the natural
fitness of things, to "go and slumber again." I will
not attempt to decide which of those three possible
causes is the true one; but so much is certain: even
those who kick most vigorously at the rice-table, lay
them down with lamb-like meekness to the siesta. I
confess I was very glad myself to escape into the coolness and quiet of my room. Plain enough it was, with
its bare, white-washed walls and ceiling, its red-tiled
floor and piece of coarse matting in the centre, its
cane-bottomed chairs. But how I delighted in the
absence of carpets and wall-papers, when I found the
stone floor so deliciously cool to the feet, and the bare
walls distilling a freshness as of lily-leaves! The siesta
lasted till about four. Then people began to hurry past
my window, with flying towels and beating slippers,
marching to the bath-rooms. And at five tea was
brought into the verandah.

Then began the first moderately-cool hour of the day.
A slight breeze sprang up and wandered about in the
garden, stirring the dense foliage of the waringin-tree,
and making its hundreds of pendulous air-roots to gently
sway to and fro. A shower of white blossom fluttered
down from the tanjong-branches, spreading fragrance
as it fell. And, by and by, a faint rosiness began to
soften the crude white of the stuccoed walls and colon-
nades, and to kindle the feathery little cirrus-clouds
floating high overhead, in the deep blue sky where the
great "kalongs" were already beginning to circle.

At six it was almost dark.

The loungers in the verandah rose from their tea, and
went in. And, some half-hour later, I saw the ladies
issue forth in Paris-made dresses, the men in the garb

of society accompanying them om their calls, for which
I was told this was the hour. The "front gallery" of
the hotel, a spacious hall supported on pillars, was
brillantly lit. A girl sat at the piano, accompanying herself to one of those weird, thrilling songs such as Grieg
and Jensen compose. And when I went in to the eight-
o'clock dinner, the menu for which might have been
written in any European hotel, I had some trouble in
identifying the scene with that which, earlier in the day,
had so rudely shocked my European ideas.  I half believed the rice-table, the sarongs and kabayas, and the
Javanese "boys" must have been a dream, until I was
convinced of the contrary by the sight of a lean brown
hand thrust out to change my plate of fish for a helping
of asparagus.

# THE TOWN

It is only for want of a better word that one uses this term of "town" to designate that picturesque ensemble of villa-studded parks and avenues, Batavia. There is, it is true, an older Batavia, grey, grim and stony as any war-scarred city of Europe—the stronghold, which the steel-clad colonists of 1620 built on the ruins of burnt-down Jacatra. But, long since abandoned by soldiers and peaceful citizens alike, and its once stately mansions degraded to offices and warehouses, it has sunk into a mere suburb—the business quarter of Batavia— alive during a few hours of the day only, and sinking back into a death-like stillness, as soon as the rumble of the last down-train has died away among its echoing streets. And the real Batavia—in contradistinction to which this ancient quarter is called "the town"—is as unlike it as if it had been built by a different order of beings.

It is best described as a system of parks and avenues, linked by many a pleasant byway and shadowy path, with here and there a glimpse of the Kali Batawi gliding along between the bamboo groves on its banks, and everywhere the whiteness of low, pillared houses, standing well back from the road, each in its own leafy garden.

Instead of walls, a row of low stone pillars, not much higher than milestones, separates private from public grounds, so that from a distance one cannot see where the park ends and the street begins. The shadow of the tall trees in the avenue keeps the garden cool, and the white dust of the road is sprinkled with the flowers that lie scattered over the smooth grass-plots and shell-strewn paths of the villa.

Among the squares of Batavia, the largest and most remarkable by far is the famous Koningsplein. It is not so much a square as simply a field, vast enough to build a city on, dotted from place to place by pasturing cattle, and bordered on the four sides of its irregular quadrangle by a triple row of branching tamarinds. From the southern distance two aerial mountain-tops overlook it. The brown bare expanse of meadowy ground, lying thus broadly open to the sky, with nothing but clouds and cloudlike hill-tops rising above its distant rampart of trees, seems like a tract of untamed wilderness, strangely set in the midst of a city, and all the more savage and lonely for these smooth surroundings. Between the stems of the delicate-leaved tamarinds, glimpses are caught of gateways and pillared houses; the eastern side of the quadrangle is disfigured by a glaring railway-station; and notwithstanding, it remains a rugged solitary spot, a waste, irreclaimably barren, which, by the sheer strength of its unconquered wildness, subdues its environment to its own mood. The houses, glinting between the trees, seem mere accidents of the landscape, simply heaps of stones; the glaring railway-station itself sinks into an indistinct whiteness, dissociated from any idea of human thought and enterprise.

Now and then a native traverses the field, slowly

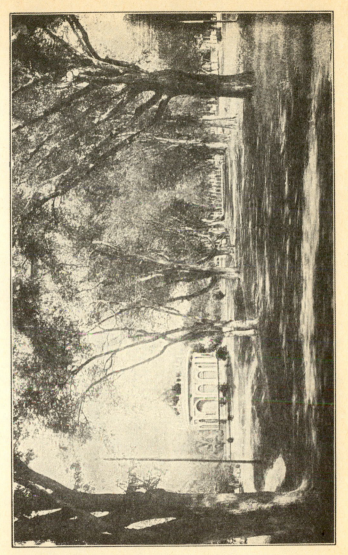

„A triple row of branching tamarinds."

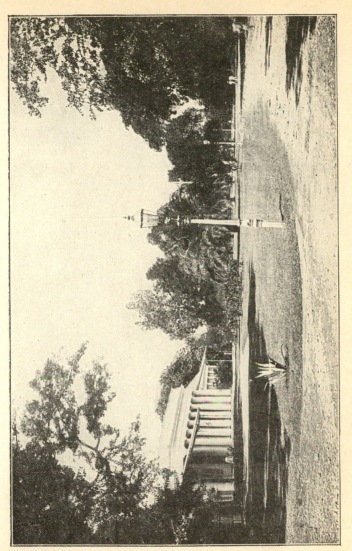

"The idyllic Duke's park, very shadowy fragrant, and green."

moving along an invisible track. He does not disturb
the loneliness. He is indigenous to the place, its natural
product, almost as much as the cicadas trilling among
the grass-blades, the snakes darting in and out among
the crevices of the sun-baked soil, and the lean cattle,
upon whose backs the crows perch. There is but one
abiding power and presence here—the broad brown
field under the broad blue sky, shifting shades and
splendours over it, and that horizon of sombre trees
all around.

This vast sweep of sky gives the Plein a tone and
atmosphere of its own. The changes in the hour and
the season that are but guessed at from some occasional
glimpse in the street, are here fully revealed. The light
may have been glaring enough among the whitewashed
houses of Ryswyk and Molenvliet—it is on the Plein
only that tropical sunshine manifests itself in the plen-
itude of its power. The great sun stands flaming in the
dizzy heights; from the scorched field to the incandescent
zenith the air is one immense blaze, a motionless flame
in which the tall tamarinds stand sere and grey, the
grass shrivels up to a tawny hay, and the bare soil
stiffens and cracks.—The intolerable day is past. People,
returning home from the town, see a roseate sheen
playing over roofs and walls, a long crimson cloud
sailing high overhead. Those walking on the Plein
behold an apocalyptic heaven and a transfigured earth,
a firmamental conflagration, eruptions of scarlet flame
through incarnadined cloud, runnels of fire darting
across the melting gold and translucent green of the
horizon; hill-tops changed into craters and tall trees
into fountains of purple light. And many are the nights,
when, becoming aware of a dimness in the moonlit air,
I have hastened to the Koningsplein, and found it whitely

waving with mist, a very lake of vapour, fitfully heaving and sinking in the uncertain moonlight, and rolling airy waves against a shore of darkness.

The seasons, too—how they triumph in this bit of open country! When, after the devouring heat of the East monsoon, the good gift of the rains is poured down from the heavens, and the town knows of nothing but

"The business-quarter of Batavia"

impracticable streets, flooded houses, and crumbling walls, it is a time of resurrection and vernal glory for the Plein. The tamarinds, gaunt gray skeletons a few days ago, burst into full-leaved greenness; the hard, white, cracked soil is suddenly covered with tender grass, fresh, as the herbage of an April meadow under western skies. In the early morning, the broad young blades are white with dew. There is a thin silvery haze in the air, which dissolves into a pink and golden radiance, as the first slanting sunbeams pierce it. And the tree-tops, far off and indistinct, seem to rise airily over hollows of blue shade.

Not far from the Koningsplein there is another square,

"A footsore Klontong trudging wearily along."

its very opposite in aspect and character—the idyllic Duke's Park very shadowy fragrant and green. One walks in it as in a poet's dream. All around there is the multitudinous budding and blossoming of many-coloured flowers, a play of transparent bamboo-shadows that flit and shift over smooth grassplot and shell-strewn path, a ceaseless alternation of glooms and glories. Set amidst tall dark trees, whose topmost branches break out into a flame of blossom, there stands a withe pillared building, palace-like in the severe grace of its architecture. Is it the Renaissance style of those gleaming columns and marble steps, or that name of "the Duke's Park," or both, that stir up the fancy to thoughts of some six-teenth-century Italian pleasaunce, such as Shakspeare loved as a setting for his love-stories? A Duke as gentle as his prince of Illyria, Olivia's sighing lover, might have walked these glades, listening to disguised Viola as, all unsuspectedly, she wooed him from his forlorn alle-giance.

The irony of facts has willed it otherwise.

A duke it was, sure enough, who stood sponsor to the spot. But as (according to French authorities) there are fagots and fagots, even so there are Dukes and Dukes—and vastly more points of difference than of resemblance between Viola's gentle prince, and the thunderous old Lord of Saxen-Weimar, to whose rum-bling Kreuzdonnerwetters and Himmel-Sakraments this abode of romance re-echoed some fifty years ago. A distant relative to the King of the Netherlands, he was indebted to his Royal kinsman's sense of family-duty for these snug quarters, a very considerable income (from the National Treasury) and the post of an Army Commander, which upheld the prince in the pensioner. His tastes were few and simple, and saving the one delight of his soul, a penurious youth, and the hardships of the Napoleonic supremacy having so thoroughly taught him the habit, that it had become a second nature to him; and would not be ousted now by the mere fact of his having become rich. He was proud of his parsimony too, prouder even than of his swearing, remarkable as it was; and, amidst the pomp and circumstance he had so late in life attained to, neglected not the humble talents which had solaced his less affluent days. So that, looking upon the many goodly acres around his palace, lying barren of all save grass, flowers, blossoming trees, and such like useless stuff, he at once saw what an unique opportunity it would

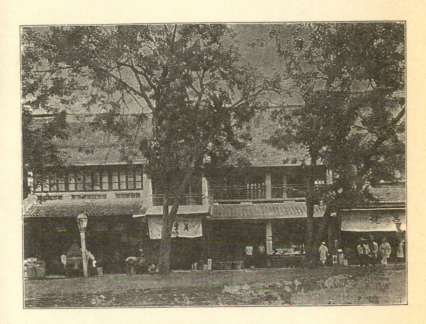

The Chinese quarter.

afford him for the exercise of his favourite virtue. And, setting about the matter in his own thorough-going way, he cut down the trees, ploughed up the grassplots, and had the grounds neatly laid out in onion-beds, and plantations of the sirih, which the Javanese loves. Here one might meet the Duke of a morning—a portly, bald-pated, red-faced old warrior with a prodigious "meer-schaum" protruding from his bristling white beard, stars, crosses, and goldlace all over his general's uniform, and a pair of list slippers on his rheumatic old toes. An orderly walked behind him, holding a gold-edged sunshade over his shining pate. And every now and then, the Duke would stop to look earnestly at his crops; and stooping with a groaning of his flesh, and

"The West-monsoon has set in, flooding the town."

a creaking of his tight tunic, straighten some trailing plant, or flick an insect off the sirih leaves.

> "The Duke was in his kitchen-garden,
>     A counting of his money."

as one might vary the nursery-rhyme.

For money it was he counted, when he gazed so long and earnestly at his vegetables—the alchemy of his thrifty imagination turning every young stalk and sprouting leaflet into a bit of metal, adorned with his Royal kinsman's effigy. And when the green penniesto-be were plentiful, well content was the gardener; and if not—"Mountains and vales and floods, heard *Ye* those oaths?" Tradition has kept an echo of them. They were something quite out of the common order, and with a style and sound so emphatically their own as to

"The Kali Batawi on its way through the Chinese quarter."

baffle imitation, and render description a hopeless task. Nor did this originality wear off, as in the course of time, the worthy Duke began to forget the language of the Fatherland. For, losing his German, he found not his Dutch, and the expressions he composed out of such odds and ends of the two languages, as he could lay

tongue to, would have astonished the builders of Babel
Tower. Fortunately, however, his anger was as short-
lived as it was violent, and, when the last thunderclap
of Kreuzmillionen Himmels Donnerwetter had gradually
died away in an indistinct grumbling, he would summon
his attendant for a light to rekindle his pipe with a
"come now, thou black pigdog" that sounded quite
friendly. A kind-hearted old blusterer at bottom, he
treated his dependents well and never sent away a
beggar pennyless. "Doitless" I should have written, for
his donations never exceeded that amount.

There is a tale of an A. D. C., his appointed almoner
for the time, having one day come to him with a sub-
scription-list on which the customary "doit" figured as
His Serene Highness the Duke of Saxen Weimar's con-
tribution; and hinting at what he considered the dis-
proportion between the exiguity of the gift, and the
wealth and worldly station of the giver. He must have
been a very rash A. D. C. The Duke turned upon him
like a savage bull. And after a volley of oaths: "Too
little!" he roared: "Too little!" and again, "Too little!
I would have you know, younker! that a "doit" is a great
deal when one has nothing at all!"

It was a cry de profundis—laughable and half con-
temptible as it sounded, the echo from unforgotten
depths of misery.

He had known what it meant "to have nothing at
all." Wherefore, and for those winged words in which
he uttered the knowledge, let his onion-beds be forgiven
him. Of the outrage he committed, only the memory
is left—the effects have long since been obliterated:
bountiful tropical nature having again showered her
treasures of leaf and flower over the beggared garden,
and re-erected in their places the green towers of her trees.

Rijswijk, Noordwijk and Molenvliet, the commercial quarters of Batavia, are more European in aspect than the Koningsplein; the houses—shops for the most part—are built in straight rows; a pavement borders the streets, and a noisy little steam-car pants and rattles

Entrance to a rich Chinaman's house.

past from morning till night. But, with these European traits, Javanese characteristics mingle, and the resulting effects is a most curious one, somewhat bewildering withal to the new-comer in its mixture of the unknown with the familiar. Absolutely commonplace-shops are

approached through gardens, the pavement is strewn
with flowers of the flame-of-the-forest : and at the street-
corners, instead of cabs, one finds the nondescript sadoo,
its driver, gay in a flowered muslin vest and a gaudy
headkerchief, squatting cross-legged on the back seat.
Noordwijk is unique, an Amsterdam-"gracht" in a
tropical setting. Imagine a long straight canal, a gleam
of green-brown water between walls of reddish masonry
—spanned from place to place by a bridge, and shaded
by the softly-tinted leafage of tamarinds ; on either side
a wide, dusty road, arid gardens, sweltering in the sun,
and glaring white bungalows; the fiery blue of the
tropical sky over it all. Gaudily-painted "praos" glide
down the dark canal; native women pass up and down
the flight of stone steps that climbs from the water's
edge to the street, a flower stuck into their gleaming
hair, still wet from the bath; the tribe of fruitvendors
and sellers of sweet drinks and cakes have established
themselves along the parapet, in the shade of the
tamarinds; and the native crowd, coming and going all
day long, makes a kaleidoscopic play of colours along
the still dark water.

From the little station at the corner of Noordwijk
and Molenvliet, a steam-car runs along the canal down
to the suburbs; every quarter of an hour it comes past,
puffing and rattling; and every time the third-class
compartment is choking full of natives. The fever and
the fret of European life have seized upon these leisurely
Orientals too. They have abandoned their sirih-chewing
and day-dreaming upon the square of matting in the
cool corner of the house, the dusty path along which
they used to trudge in Indian file, when there was an
urgent necessity for going to market; and behold them
all perched upon this "devil's engine," where they cannot

"A glimpse of the river as it glides along between the bamboo groves of its margins."

even sit down in the way they were taught to, „hurkl-ing on their hunkers."

The skippers and raftsmen are more conservative in their ways—owing, perhaps, to their constant commu-nion with the deliberate stream, which saunters along on its way from the hills to the sea, at its own pace. They take life easily; paddling along over the shifting shallows and mud-banks of the Kali (river) in the same leisurely way their forbears did; conveying red tiles, bricks and earthenware in flat-bottomed boats; or pushing along rafts of bamboo-stems, which they have felled in the wood up-stream. As they come floating down the canal, these rafts of green bamboo, with the thin tips curving upwards like tails and stings of ven-omous insects, have a fantastical appearance of living, writhing creatures, which the native raftsman seems to be for ever fighting with his long pole. After dark, when the torch at the prow blazes out like the single baleful eye of the monstrous thing, the dray-dream deepens into a nightmare. And shuddering, one remembers ghastly legends of river-dragons and serpents that haunt the sea, swimming up-stream to ravish some wretched mortal.

The native boats appeal to merrier thoughts. With the staring white-and-black goggle eyes painted upon the prow, and the rows of red, yellow and green lozenges arranged like scales along the sides, they remind one irresistibly of grotesque fishes for those big children, the Javanese, to play with—at house-keeping. For keep house they do in their boats. They eat, drink, sleep, and live in the prao. A roof of plaited bamboo-leaves helps to make the stern into the semblance of a hut; and here, whilst the owner pushes along the floating home by means of a long pole and a deal of apparent exertion, his wife sits cooking the rice for the family-meal over a brazier full of live coals; and the children tumble about in happy nakedness. Javanese babies, by the way, always seem happy. What do they amuse themselves with, one wonders? They do not seem to know any games, and playthings they have none, except the tanjong-flowers they make necklaces of, and perchance some luckless cockroach, round whose hindmost leg they tie a thread to make him walk the way he should. Their parents, Mohammedan orthodoxy debars them from the society of their natural companions—dogs; and, as for cats, that last resource of unamused childhood in Europe, they hold them sacred, and would not dare to lay a playful hand upon one of them. Yet, there they are—plaything-less, naked and supremely happy.

Their parents, for the matter of that, are exactly the same; they seem perfectly happy without any visible and adequate cause for such content. As long as they are not dying—and one sometimes doubts if Javanese die at all—all is well with them. The race has a special genius for happiness, the free gift of those same inscrutable powers who have inflicted industry, moral sense, and the overpowering desire for clothes upon the unfortunate nations of the North.

Following the left-ward bend of the canal, past the sluice, and the Post Office,—the most hideous structure by the bye that ever disfigured a decent street—one comes to the bridge of Kampong Bahru; and crossing it, suddenly finds oneself in what seems another quarter of the globe. Tall, narrow houses, quaintly decorated and crowned with red-tiled roofs, that flame out against the contrasting azure of the sky, stand in close-built rows; the wide street is full of jostling carts and vans, fairly humming with traffic; and the people move with

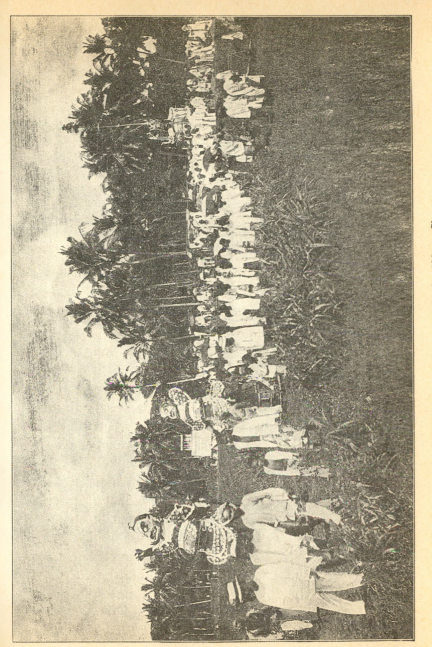

Funeral Procession on its way to the Chinese Cimetry.

THE TOWN 51

an energy and briskness never seen among Javanese. This is the Chinese quarter. There are three or four such in the town, inhabited by Chinese exclusively. This habit of herding together—though now a matter of choice with the Celestials—is the survival of a tim when Batavia had its "camp" as mediæval Italian cities had their Ghetto: a period no further back than the beginning of the last century.

At that time, when Chinese immigration threatened to become a danger to the colony, the then Governor-General, Valckenier, took some measures against the admittance of destitute Chinese, which, however well-designed, were so clumsily executed as to spread the rumour that the Government intended to deport even the Chinese residents of Batavia. A panic broke out among them, and then a revolt, in which they were soon joined by their countrymen from all over the island. After a desperate struggle, atrocities innumerable both suffered and inflicted, a siege sustained, and an attack of fifty and odd thousand beaten back by their two thousand men, the Hollanders succeeded in putting down the rebellion, and the enemy fled to the woods and swamps of the lowlands around Batavia. A few months later however, a general amnesty having been granted, such of them as had escaped from famine and jungle-fever returned, and a special quarter was assigned to them, where it would be easy both to protect and to control them. There they have since continued to live.

The houses of some rich Chinamen in the Kampong Bahru-neighbourhood are truly splendid; the most modest ones still have an air of comfort. According to the ideas of the inhabitants, there are none absolutely squalid. All these houses are at the same time shops. They are, in a way, wonderful people, these sons of the

Celestial Empire, merchants in one way or other, all of
them. There is of course a difference. There is the
foot-sore "klontong" trudging through the wearey strets
all day, and shaking his rattle as he goes, to advertise
the reels of cotton and the cakes of soap in his wallet;
and again there is the portly millionaire, who entertains
army officers and civil servants in his own profusely-
decorated mansion; but the difference is one in degree
only, not in kind. Amid the pomp and circumstance of
the one condition and the squalor of the other, the
individualities are the same, the attitude of mind and
the habits of thought identical, the sum and substance
of a Chinaman's life in Java being expressed in "the
making of bargains". He could as soon leave off breath-
ing as leave of buying and selling; trading seems to be
his natural function. And this, one fancies, is the great
difference between his race and ours; and the true secret
of their superiority as money-makers. A Caucasian, if
he is a merchant, is so with a certain part of his being
only—during certain hours of the day, in his own office.
A Chinaman is a merchant with his whole heart, his
whole soul and his whole understanding, a merchant
always and everywhere, from his cradle to his grave,
at table, at play, over his opium-pipe, in his temple.
Trade is the element in which he lives, moves, and has
his being. His thoughts might be noted in figures. The
world is to him one vast opportunity for making money,
and all things in it are articles of trade; which, in
Chinese, means gain to him and loss to everybody else.
He has few wants, infinite resources, and the faith (in
himself) that removeth trading towns. Small wonder
if he succeeds.

I fancy it would be quite a practical education in
the principles of business, to watch the career of one

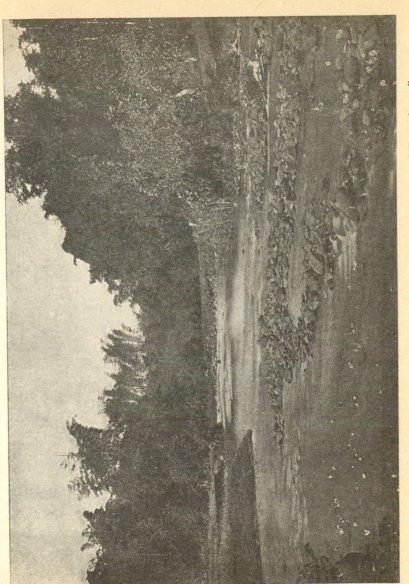

"The deliberate stream sauntering along at its own pace on its way from the hills to the sea".

of these Chinamen, from the hour of his arrival at Tanjong Priok onward. At first, you see him trudging along with a wallet, containing soap, sewing cotton, combs and matches. After a few months, you find him in your compound surrounded by the whole of your domestic staff, to whom he is selling sarong-cloth and thin silks. When a year has gone by, a coolie trudges at his heels panting under a load of wares, the samples of which he subjects to your approval with the most correct of bows. Have but patience, and you will find him in a diminutive shop, where somehow he finds place for a settee in the corner, a mirror on the wall, and all around such a collection of articles as might fitly be termed an epitome of material civilization. Nor does he stop in that tiny shop. A few years later he will be taking his ease behind the counter of a spick-and-span establishment in the camp; and if by chance you get a glimpse of his wife, you will be astonished at the size of the diamonds in her shiny coil of hair. Our friend is on the high road to prosperity now, which leads to a big house separate from the shop. Before he is fairly fifty, he has built it, high and spacious, with an altar to the gods and to the spirits of his ancestors set in the midst of it, and a profusion of fine carving and gilding, of embroidered hangings and lacquered woodwork all around. He will invite you for the New Year's festivities now, and if your wife accompanies you, introduce you to his spouse, resplendent as the rainbow in many-tinted brocades, and more thickly covered with diamonds than the untrodden meadow with the dews of a midsummer night. He talks about the funeral of his honoured father, which cost him upward of three thousand pounds sterling; and he will ask your advice over the pine-apples and the champagne,

about sending his son to Europe in one oɪ his own
ships, that the youth may see something of the world,
and if he so list, be entered as a student at the famous
university of Leijden.

# A COLONIAL HOME

"It is the North which has introduced tight-fitting clothes and high houses." Thus Taine as, in the streets of Pompeii, he gazed at nobly-planned peristyle and graceful arch, at godlike figures shining from frescoed walls, and with the vision of that fair, free, large life of antiquity, contrasted the Paris apartment from which he was but newly escaped, and the dress-coat which he had worn at the last social function. And a similar reflection crosses the Northerner's mind when the looks upon a house in Batavia.

I am aware that Pompeii and Batavia, pronounced in one breath, make a shrieking discord, and that, between a homely white-washed bungalow and those radiant mansions which the ancients built of white marble and blue sky, the comparison must seem preposterous. And yet, no one can see the two, and fail to make it. The resemblance is too striking. The flat roof, the pillared entrance, the gleam of the marble-paved hall, whose central arch opens on the reposeful shadow of the inner chambers, all these features of a

classic dwelling are recognized in a Batavia house.
Evidently too, this resemblance is not the result of
mere mechanical imitation.   There are a consistency
and thoroughness in the architecture of these houses, a
harmony with the surrounding landscape, which stamp
it as an indigenous growth, the necessary result of the
climate, and the mode of life in Java, just as classic
architecture was the necessary result of the climate and
the mode of life in Greece and Italy.  If the two styles
are similar, it is because the ideas which inspired them
are not so vastly different. After all, in a sunny country,
whether it be Europe or Asia, the great affair of
physical life is to keep cool, and the main idea of the
architect, in consequence will be to provide that coolness.   It is this which constitutes a resemblance between
countries in all other respects so utterly unlike as Greece
and Java, and the difference between these and Northern
Europe.   In the North, the human habitation is a fortress against the cold; in the South and the East, it is
a shelter from the heat.

There is no need here of thick walls, solid doors,
casements of impermeable material, all the barricades
which the Northerner throws up against the besieging
elements. In Italy, as in Greece, Nature is not inimical.
The powers of sun, wind, and rain are gracious to
living things, and under their benign rule man lives as
simply and confidingly as his lesser brethren, the beasts
of the fields and forests, and the birds of the air. He
has no more need than they to hedge in his individual
existence from the vast life that encompasses it.  His
clothes, when he wears them, are an ornament rather
than a protection, and his house a place, not of refuge,
but of enjoyment, a cool and shadow spot, as open to
the breeze as the forest, whose flat spreading branches,

"Compound" of a Batavia house.

supported on stalwart stems, seem to have been the model for its column-borne roof.

The Batavia house, then, is built on the classic plan. Its entrance is formed by a spacious loggia, raised a few steps above the level ground, and supported on columns. Thence, a door, which stands open all day long, leads into a smaller inner hall, on either side of which are bedrooms, and behind this is another loggia —even more spacious than the one forming the entrance of the house—where meals are taken and the hot hours of the day are spent. Generally, a verandah runs around the whole building, to beat off both the fierce sunshine of the hot, and the cataracts of rain of the wet season. Behind the house is a garden, enclosed on three sides by the buildings containing the servants' quarters, the kitchen and store rooms, the bath-rooms and stables. And at some distance from the main building and connected with it by a portico, stands a pavilion, for the accommodation of guests;—for the average Netherlands-Indian is the most hospitable of mortals, and seldom without visitors, whether relatives, friends, or even utter strangers, who have come with an introduction from a common acquaintance in Holland.

It takes some time, I find, to get quite accustomed to this arrangement of a house. In the beginning of my stay here, I had an impression of always being out of doors and of dining in the public street, especially at night, when in the midst of a blaze of light one felt oneself an object of attention and criticism to every chance passer-by in the darkness without. It was as bad as at the ceremonious meals of the Kings of France, who had their table laid out in public, that their faithful subjects might behold them at the banquet, and, one supposes, satisfy their own hunger by the Sovereign's vicarious dining.

In time however, as the strangeness of the situation wears off, one realises the advantage of these spacious galleries to walled-in rooms, and very gladly sacrifices the sentiment of privacy to the sensation of coolness.

For to be cool, or not to be cool, that is the great question, and all things are arranged with a view to solving it in the most satisfactory manner possible. For the sake of coolness, one has marble floors or Javanese matting instead of carpets, cane-bottomed chairs and settees in lieu of velvet-covered furniture, gauze hangings for draperies of silks and brocade. The inner hall of almost every house, it is true, is furnished in European style—exiles love to surround themselves with remembrances of their far-away home. But, though very pretty, this room is generally empty of inhabitants, except perhaps, for an hour now and then, during the rainy season. For in this climate, to sit in a velvet chair is to realize the sensations of Saint Laurence, without the sustaining consciousness of martyrdom.— For the sake of coolness again, one gets up at half-past five or six, at the very latest, keeps indoors till sunset, sleeps away the hot hours of the afternoon on a bed which it requires experience and a delicate sense of touch to distinguish from a deal board, and spends the better part of one's waking existence in the bath-room.

Now, a bath in Java is a very different thing from the dabbling among dishes in a bedroom, which Europeans call by that name, even if their dishes attain the dimensions of a tub. Ablutions such as these are performed as a matter of duty; a man gets into his tub as he gets into his clothes, because to omit doing so would be indecent. But bathing in the tropics is a pure delight, a luxury for body and soul—a dip into the *Fontaine de Jouvence*, almost the "cheerful solemnity and semi-pagan act of worship," which the donkey-driving Traveller through the Cevennes performed in the clear Tarn. A special

The servants' kitchen.

place is set apart for it, a spacious, cool, airy room in the outbuildings, a "chamber deaf to noise, and all but blind to light." Through the gratings over the door, a glimpse of sky and waving branches is caught. The marble floor and whitewashed walls breathe freshness, the water in the stone reservoir is limpid and cold as that of a pool that gleams in rocky hollows. And as the bather dips in his bucket, and send the frigid stream pouring over him, he washes away, not heat and dust alone, but weariness and vexatious thought in a purification of both body and soul, and he understands why all Eastern creeds have exalted the bath into a religious observance.

Like the often-repeated bath, the rice-table is a Javanese institution, and its apologists claim equal honours for it as an antidote to climatic influences. I confess I do not hold so high an opinion of its virtues, but I have fallen a victim to its charms. I love it but too well. And there lies the danger, everybody likes it far too much, and especially, likes far too much of it. It is, humanly speaking, impossible to partake of the rice table, and not to grossly overeat oneself. There is something insidious about its composition, a cunning arrangement of its countless details into a whole so perfectly harmonious that it seems impossible to leave out a single one. If you have partaken of one dish, you must partake of the rest, unless you would spoil all. Fowl calls to fowl, and fish answers fish, and all the green things that are on the table, aye, and the red and the yellow likewise, have their appointed places upon your plate. You may try to escape consequences by taking infinitesimal pinches of each, but many a mickle makes a muckle, and your added teaspoonfuls soon swell to a heaped-up plate, such as well might stagger the stoutest appetite. Yet, even before you have recovered from your surprise, you find you have finished it all. I do not pretend to explain, I merely state the fact.

Records have survived of those Pantagruelic feasts with which the great ones of the mediæval world delighted to celebrate the auspicious events of their lives, and the chronicler never fails to sum up the almost interminable list of the spices and essences with which the cook, on the advice of learned physicians, seasoned the viands, in order that, whilst the grosser meats satisfied the animal cravings of the stomach, those ethereal aromatics might stimulate the finer fluids, whose ebb and flow controls the soul, and the well-flavoured dishes might not only be hot on men's tongues but eke "prick them in their courages." They pricked to some purpose, it seems. And if the spice-sated Netherlands-Indian is a comparatively law-abiding man, it must be because battening rice counteracts maddening curry. But for this providential arrangement, I fully believe he would think no more of battle, murder, and sudden death than of an indigestion, and consider a good dinner as an ample explanation of both.

Now, as to what they clothe themselves withal. Taine's opinion concerning tight fitting clothes has been mentioned—viz: that they are an invention of the North. A fortnight in Batavia will explain and prove the theory better than many books by many philosophers; and moreover, cause the most sartorially-minded individual to consign the "invention" to a place hotter than even Java. Like the habitations, the habits of European civilization are irksome in the tropics; and, for indoor-wear at least, they have suffered a sun-change into something cool and strange—into native costume modified in fact. Now, the outward apparel of the Javanese consists of a long straight narrow skirt "the sarong" with a loose fitting kind of jacket over it,—short for the men, who call it "badjoo," and longer for the women

who wear it as "kabaya": which garments have been
adopted by the Hollanders, with the one modification
of the sarong into a "divided skirt" for the men, and
the substitution of white batiste and embroidery for the
coloured stuffs of which native women make their
kabayas, in the case of the ladies. On the Javanese, a
small, spare, slightly-made race, the garb sits not un-
gracefully; narrow and straight as it is, it goes well with
contours so attenuated. But on the sturdier Hollander
the effect is something appalling. An adequate description of the men's appearance in it would read like a
caricature; and though, with the help of harmonious
colours and jewellery, the women look better when
thus attired, the dress is not becoming to them either,
at least in non-colonial eyes. The æsthetic sense shies
and kicks out at the sight of those straight, hard, un-
natural lines. Modern male costume has been held up
to ridicule as a "system of cylinders". The sarong and
kabaya combine to form one single cylinder, which
obliterates all the natural lines and curves of the feminine
form divine and changes a woman into a parti-coloured
pillar, for an analogy to which one's thoughts revert to
Lot's wife. But, though utterly condemned from an
artistic point of view, from a practical one it must be
acquitted, and even commended. In a country where
the temperature ranges between 85° and 95° Fahrenheit
in the shade, cool clothes which can be changed several
times a day, are a condition not merely of comfort, but
of absolute cleanliness and decency, not to mention
hygiene. For it is a noteworthy fact that the women,
who wear colonial dress up to six in the evening, stand
the climate better than the men, who, in the course of
things, wear it during an hour or an hour and a half
at most, in the day. And it must be admitted that both

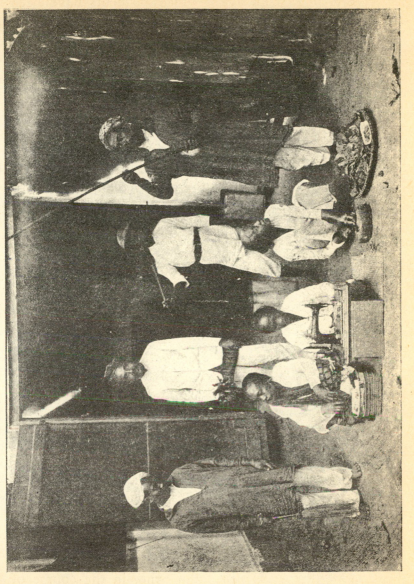

Native servants.

men and women enjoy better health in Java, under this colonial regime of dressing than in the British possessions, where they cling to the fashions of Europe.

As for the children, they are clad even more lightly than their elders, in what the Malay calls "monkey-trousers", tjelana monjet, a single garment, which, only just covering the body, leaves the neck, arms and legs bare. It is hideous, and they love it. In German picture-books one sees babes similarly accoutred riding on the stork, that brings them to their expectant parents. Perhaps, after all, monkey-trousers are the paradisiacal garment of babes; and it is a Wordsworthian recollection of this fact, that makes them cling to the costume so tenaciously.

One cannot speak of an "Indian" child, and forget the "babu," the native nurse, who is its ministering spirit, its dusky guardian angel, almost its Providence. All day long, she carries her little charge in her long "slendang," the wide scarf, which deftly slung about her shoulders, makes a sort of a hammock for the baby. She does not like even the mother to take it away from her; feeds it, bathes it, dresses it prettily, takes it out for a walk, ready, at the least sign, to lift it up again into its safe nest close to her heart. She plays with it, not as a matter of duty, but as a matter of pleasure, throwing herself into the game with enjoyment and zest, like the child she is at heart; so that the two may be seen quarrelling sometimes, the baby stamping its feet and the babu protesting with the native cluck of indignant remonstrance, and an angry "Terlalu! "it is too bad!" And at night, when she has crooned the little one to sleep, with one of those plaintive monotonous melodies in a minor key, which seem to go on for ever, like a rustling of reeds and forest leaves whilst the crickets are trilling their evensong, she spreads her piece of matting on the floor, and lies down in front of the little bed, like a faithful dog guarding its master's slumbers.

As for the other servants, their name is Legion. A colonial household requires a very numerous domestic staff. Even families with modest incomes employ six or seven servants, and ten is by no means an exceptional number. The reason for this apparent extravagance is, that, though the Javanese is not lazy—as he often and unjustly is accused of being—yet he is so slow, that the result practically is the same, and one needs two or even three native servants, for work which one Caucasian would despatch in the same time.

All these have their own quarters in the "compound" and their own families in those quarters; they go "into the house" as a man would go to his office; coming home for meals, and entertaining their friends in the evening, on their own square of matting, and with their own saffron-tinted rice, and syrup-sweetened coffee.

Such then is the setting of every-day existence in Java.

As for the central fact, it is less interesting than its circumstances, in so far as it is more familiar. The three or four great conceptions which determine the home-life of a people—its ideas social, ethical, and religious concerning the relations between parent and child and between men and women—are too deeply ingrained into its mental substance to be affected by any merely outward circumstances. Therefore, home-life among the Hollanders in Java, is essentially the same as among Hollanders in their own country. Still there is difference, that it has more physical comfort and less intellectual interest. The climate, it seems to me, is in a high degree responsible for both these facts.

A continual temperature of about 90 degrees is not favourable to the growth of the finer faculties, in Northerner's brains at least. The little band of eminent men who have gone up from Java to shine in Dutch

Native gardener.

Universities must be regarded as a signal exception to a very general rule. Besides, the heat is so grave an addition to the already heavy burden of the day, that one requires all one's energies, both of body and soul, to conscientiously discharge one's ordinary duties;

and there is no surplus left to devote to literary, artistic, or scientific pursuits. There are no theatres, no operas, no concerts, no lectures, no really good newspapers even, in Java. There could not be, where there is so little active public life. So that a man's one relaxation after a hard day's work—unless he looks at dances and dinners in that light—must be found in his own house.

One continually hears the phrase in the East: "our house is our life." Naturally therefore, the house is made as pleasant as possible, and as comfortable, not to say luxurious. Incomes are proportionately very much higher in Java than in Holland—without financial advantage as an incentive, nobody would accept life under tropical conditions—and the better part of the money is spent on good living in the majority of cases. Even families of comparatively moderate means have a roomy house, a sufficient domestic staff, and keep a carriage and a good table.

And as to the heat, which assuredly is a discomfort, and no trifling one, the accepted mode of life does much to palliate it, not only by the regime of housing, feeding and dressing, but almost as much by the way the day is divided. Work is begun early, so as to get as much as possible done in the cool hours; between nine and five everybody keeps indoors; and those who can snatch an hour of leisure after the one o'clock rice-table, spend it in a siesta. Only in the early morning and in the evening does one see Europeans about. Not even the greatest enthusiast for cricket and tennis dare begin games earlier than half-past four.

Formerly this was different.

On old engravings, one may see the tall sombre houses which the first colonists built on those "grachts" now long since demolished. One may mark them

walking home from a three hours' sermon in broadcloth
mantles and velvet robes, giving solemn entertainments
in their trim gardens along the canal, with the sun in
noon-day glory over-head, and generally ignoring the

Native footboy.

trifling differences between Amsterdam and Batavia.
They fought very valiantly for their ancestral customs;
but very few returned to tell of the fight.

Since, people have reflected that a live Netherlands-
Indian is better then a dead Hollander. And giving

up a fight, in which defeat was all but certain, and success worse than useless, they have effected a compromise with the climate. In Java they do as Java does, from sunrise to sunset. But with the congenial cool of the evening, they resume their national existence, the garb, the manners and the customs of Holland. At seven there is a general "va et vient" of open carriages bearing women in light dresses and men in correct black-and-white to a "reception" in some brilliantly-lighted house; and for a few hours, the life of Home is lived again.

Outside is the black tropical night, heavy with the scent of invisible blossoms, pricked here and there by the yellow spark of some trudging fruitvendor's oilwick. The small fragment of Europe which that tall-colonnaded marble-paved loggia, with its gliding figures of men and women, is, stands an Island of Light among the waveless seas of darkness.

Sacred gun near the Amsterdam gate, Batavia.

# SOCIAL LIFE

The social life of Batavia has a physiognomy of its own; curious enough in some of its features. But it is not this which strikes the new-comer most forcibly. In certain Byzantine mosaics, the figure represented is entirely eclipsed by the magnificence of the background: the eye must grow accustomed to the splendour of the gold and precious stones surrounding it, before it can take in the lines of the face. In a similar manner, no surmise can be formed as to the character of Batavia-social life before the charm has, at least in part, passed off, which its setting casts over the critical faculties. It moves in romance; it is surrounded by beauty; its conditions and circumstances are in themselves a source of delight. It would seem almost enough for a feast in the cool of the evening, to sit under the verandah, marking on the gleaming marble floor half-reflections as in tranquil waters under a tranquil sky seen from afar; and the rich strange green, relieved against blackness, of the plants on the steps outside, their every leaf and shoot shone upon by the lamplight, standing out sparkling against the ebon wall of night. From without there comes the chirping of crickets, and the deep-breathed fragance of flowers—-tuberose, gardenia and datura, nocturnal blossoms. Framed between pillars and architrave, great rectangles of sky are seen, interstellar azure and the countless scintillation of stars. Environings such as these shed a grace and dignity even over the actions of daily life. When the scene is in itself fair, it is transfigured into what seems the vision of a poet.

Shortly after my arrival, I was invited to a ball at the palace. I was at the time staying with friends in the Salemba quarter; and we had a drive of nearly an hour through avenues of tall waringin trees. There was no wind, not the faintest breath of air; all that world of leaves stood unstirred; summits broad as hilltops, and cascades of massive foliage, making a blackness against skies all limpid with diffused starlight. Between the vaguely-discerned stems, the little lights, which fruit-vendors keep twinkling all the night through, would now and then flare up, and a reddish arm be revealed, the portion of a face, and some fruits in a basket. Once too, we saw the shining of a fire with some native watchmen crouching around it, their faces strangely distorted in the ever-writhing and shifting light. One of them shouted out a hoarse "who goes there?" That was the only sound I heard all the time. Silence and night all around; and overhead, like some pale river winding along, between shores of darkness, the gleaming course of the sky between the dark waringin-tops. We might have been in the heart of a woodland, miles away from the populous city, when suddenly the horses turned a corner, and there burst upon us the great white blaze of the palace, shining beyond intervening darknesses. It seemed like a low-hanging lightning-cloud, with myriads of little flames, like sparks of Saint-Elmo's fire hovering around, above, and underneath. Those aloft hung im-

movable: the steadfast stars; lower down, immovable
too, a wide-swung circle of seemingly larger luminaries
defining a tract of darkness; within that flame-bound
space, trembling hither and thither, fitful will-o'-the
wisps; and without the shining boundary, rushing lights
that darted by and suddenly stood, and then with jerks
and stops drew ever nearer to the great effulgent cloud.
Tho lights of stars, lanterns, oil-wicks, and carriage-
lamps seemed all to have been scattered from that central
glow. As we drew nearer, its cloudlike aspect changed
to the semblance of an alabaster grotto, the fire in its
white core streaked with lines of black; and these lines
broadened and lengthened until they grew into solid
shafts; when the columns of the loggia stood revealed,
rising from the height of a marble terrace.

I ascended the white steps. I was in the very heart
of the light. The pillars, the floor, the walls and the
ceiling seemed to be made of light. And suddenly, I
had a sense of home-coming. Why, I knew all this
very well! I had known it for years, for ever so long,
ever since the time when I listened to fairy tales, and
in the beautifully-bound book—I must not touch it, and
I kept my hands behind my back to withstand the
temptation—was shown the picture of the castle where
the Sleeping Beauty lived. At night, lying wide awake
up to quite nine o'clock, I saw it as plain as could be,
growing up around the lamp, with the groundglass-shade
for a cupola. Later on, when I could read myself,
and also climb trees as the boys in the village had
taught me, sitting all through the drowsy summer
afternoons in the forked branch of an old, crooked
pear-tree, with Hans Andersen's tales on my knees, I
rebuilt the Castle on a bolder scale for the Little
Mermaiden. Alas! she was never to live there! Until,

at last, when Romeo crossed the threshold, and Juliet turned and stood at gaze, a burst of music flooded the widening halls, entwined couples moved like flowers that sway in the evening wind, and between the tall columns, I caught a glimpse of the sky and "all the little stars." Now, I had entered the palace myself. The great La France roses and the Maréchal Niel that fell in showers of gold over the edge of the marble urns, had budded in my dream-garden. The music played; and in the vast hall I knew so well, the polonaise began to unwind its slow coils, with a flash of goldlace and of diamonds, a gleaming of bare shoulders, and a wavy movement of silken trains, whose hues enriched the pale marble underfoot.... "We should move into this place, I think," said my partner.

Since then, I have been to many entertainments. It is but honest to say that at some I have enjoyed myself exceedingly, pouring rains and the croaking of frogs, almost in the house, nothwithstanding; and that at others I have felt my eyes burning with tears of suppressed yawning. It is true this has not happened often; but, when it has, not all the stars in their courses, nor all the constellations in their fixed places, could inspirit me; and the perfume of the tuberoses gave me a headache. I look at these things by gas-light now; and some of them I find curious and not altogether beautiful. One especially: the official character of social life in the best circles. It seems as if discipline regulated matters of pleasure as strictly as matters of business. A man will go to his chief's party as he would to his office of a morning, never dreaming of staying away; and imposing old ladies resent the presence of the wrong partner at a whist-table, as if it were an obstacle in their husband's career. It is as if they could not, even for one evening, forget the struggle for existence, and as if they regarded a dinner or a dance as an engagement with the enemy; a brisk assault to carry by storm some place that has long stood a regular siege—a lively skirmish in which everything that comes to hand is a weapon for either attack or self-defence. One cannot be too well equipped in this great battle of official life. Intellect is an excellent weapon, but it is not the only one; and though zeal is indispensable, it is not enough. There are too many intelligent and conscientious men jostling each other already. To pass them by, the ambitious man must be more than merely intelligent and conscientious. He must choose some special talent—any talent provided it be special. Where merits are equal, the supererogatory decides the contest. For a man at all well born and well bred, accomplishments of the social order are the easiest to acquire; besides, these seemingly futile things are in reality most important. It is the men of the world who get the good places; while stay-at-home drudges may after ten years still stay at home and drudge. Accordingly, social accomplishments are what a wise man will strive to acquire. And before anything else, let him see that he plays a good game of cards. All elderly gentlemen like cards; all chiefs of departments are eldery gentlemen; therefore all chiefs of departments like cards. Hence these many and long-drawn-out parties, where one sits at little green tables until, dear God! those very tables seem asleep, and the faint heart is all but lying still. And hence the patience and the stoical courage, with which ambitious men endure the trial. Though, to the superficial observer, they are only taking their pleasures laboriously, they take better things than their pleasure: a chance of preferment. They have heard ballads being sung and said about the man who stormed the high places with his chair for a steed and a pack of cards for shield and spear, and utterly defeated and drove out the garrison of quill-armed men. These things have been. And once upon a time, there was a Head of Department, who held the official virtues to be statistics, discipline, and cards: but the greatest of these was cards. By his play, he judged a man. A woman he did not judge at all, conceiving her to be a non-card-playing being. And a woman sitting down to a game, notwithstanding her declared and organic inability, was to him the abomination of desolation. But let young civil servants come to him! And happy that young civil servant who could, and would, and did stand up to him, and even defeat him utterly, to the greater glory of cards! For this man was a truly great soul; and he preferred the honour of the game very far indeed to his own as a player.

Still, as all roads lead to Rome, so a goodmany lead to preferment. If one great man loves cards, another is partial to a good dinner, and most affable over paté-de-foie-gras and a bottle of Burgundy. And a third—this one presumably the proud father of pretty daughters—has a predilection for dances. So that a man may choose his own path upwards; and, if he will not play, why, he may dance.

And dance they do in Batavia, with fervour and assiduity. On east-monsoon nights, when the very crickets judge it too hot for the exertion of chirping, snatches of Strauss-waltzes may be caught floating out on the heavy air; and luminous shapes be seen twirling in some brilliantly-lighted front-gallery. Out of every ten persons you meet, nine are enthusiastic waltzers;

and the fieriest fanatic of them all is sure to be a young civil servant thus "with victory and with melody" pursuing his upward path to the heights of official honours. Nothing arrests him in his career. The gallery too narrow for his evolutions does not exist. One exhausted partner after another he has led back to her mamma and the restorative champagne-cup, and his ardour is not a whit abated, though his hair seems to be sprinkled with diamond-dust and its cheeks have sunk to the pallor of that wilted lily, his collar—the last of the posy gathered at home, and thrown away drooping into a corner of the dressingroom, off the verandah. This is sublime courage, indeed. As one looks at him, one is reminded of Indian braves, who at the first outburst of the war-hoop, put on their very best paint and shiniest mocassins, and hurry to the gathering of the chiefs, there to dance the war-dance; not inelegantly, nor without hidden meaning: each prance and twirl a prophecy of scalp-wreathed triumphs.

But dancing—like virtue—may be argued to be its own reward. And as such, it but partially fits into the system of amusements considered as a means to preferment. For the triumph of the principle commend me to a reception. Each great man's day—for it is his, observe, and not his wife's—is announced before-hand in the newspapers, or printed, one in a long list, on a separate slip of paper, which you must stick up in the corner of your mirror, so that there shall be no pretext for ignorance. To make assurance doubly sure, you put a pencilmark against the name and "day" of your own particular great man. On the appointed date, as the clock strikes seven, you go. From afar you see the blaze of his front gallery; the drive shines with multitudinous carriage-lamps, and every now and

then, as another vehicle draws up, the master of the
house is seen descending the verandah-steps, to help
some lady to alight from her carriage, with grave courtesy offering her his arm to conduct her towards the
hostess. She rises, extends a welcoming hand, begs her
newly-arrived guest to be seated, and resumes a languid
conversation with the great lady at her right. Unless
indeed, the new arrival be a greater lady, in which case
the former occupant will cede to her the place of honour,
and content herself with the next. Soon, around the
big marble-topped table, the circle is drawn, one-half
of it shining like the rainbowed sky; the other black
as innermost darkness; one semi-circle of women; another of men; as strictly separated as we are taught
that the sheep and goats shall be, on a certain day. I
cannot but think that the men must be conscious of
the fact and its dire symbolism. For, as often as not,
they get up, and stand unhappily together in the farthest
corner of the verandah, and with cigars and cigarettes,
make little clouds to hide themselves from the children
of the light shining afar off, and drink sherry out
of little glasses, in deep meditation. Until, suddenly,
the booming of the eight o'clock gun breaks the spell.
Every watch is taken out of every waistcoat-pocket,
and set aright. Every countenance brightens, and the
greatest man of all—"not Lancelot, nor another,"
for his life!—catching a look from his lady sitting
mournful in her place, steps forward, and boldly claims
her for his own again. Then the others follow, the
host still conducting each fair one back to her carriage;
and in another moment the verandah is left desolate,
and that reception is a thing of the past.

Not more than two or three of the guests have
interchanged a word with either host or hostess beyond

the conventional phrases of welcome and good bye; and unless some members of the same coterie have been sitting together,—Batavia-society is as full of coteries as a pine-apple is of seeds—they have not had much conversation among themselves either. Of pleasure there has been nothing, of profit so much as may be derived from seeing and being seen. It is almost as it was at the Court of Louis XIV. Acte de présence has been made: and that is all; but, as it seems, it is enough. This is indeed a triumph of the bureaucratic principle.

In "Java"—as the Batavians call the rest of the island, in curious contradistinction to the capital—this principle rules with even greater despotism: it assumes the importance of an article of faith. Batavia, after all that "suburb of the Hague," is too much influenced by the manners and opinions of the Mother Country to be accounted a colonial town. And among the colonial ideas it is gradually discarding, is that one of the extreme importance and supereminence of office. In Holland, society metes with a different measure. And the knowledge perpetually forced on him, that the Honourable of Batavia must sink into plain Mr. Jansen or Smit of the Hague, is sobering enough to keep the vanity of even the most arrogant official within decent limits. Not to mention the fact that, among his fellow-citizens, there is a large proportion of non-officials, not at all eager to acknowledge even his temporary super-iority. But in "Java," where communication with the civilized world is much less frequent and much more difficult, old colonial notions have retained their pristine vigour. The "Resident" of a little Java-station is still very much what his predecessor, the "Merchant," was in the days of the East-India Company: a veritable little king. The gilt "payong" held over his head on official occasions seems a royal canopy, and his gold-laced uniform-cap a kingly crown in the eyes of his temporary subjects. The native chiefs revere him as their "elder brother." His own subordinates naturally look up to him. The planters, who in their transactions with the native population—bad keepers of contracts, on the whole—are dependent upon his decision, need to be and to continue on good terms with him. And when it is further taken into consideration that the social life of the station must be exactly what he chooses to make it, it will be evident why even absolutely independent persons should seek to be in his good graces. Thus the man lives in an atmosphere of adulation. If there be a lack of humour or an abundance of vanity in his composition, he will take his pseudo-royalty seriously, and strictly exact homage. But in the opposite case, and even when he is averse to it, it will be still pressed upon him. An anecdote illustrating this was told me the other day by an official, himself the object, or as he put it, the victim of this particular kind of hero-worship.

He was driving at a rapid pace, down a precipitous road, when the horse stumbled and fell, his light dog-cart was upset, and he himself flung out of the seat. He had barely recovered from the stunning fall, when he caught sight of his secretary—who had been following in his own carriage—coming bounding down the steep road like a big india-rubber ball, rolling over and over in the dust. "Hullo, Jansen! have you been upset too?"—"No, Resident," sputters the fat little man, scrambling to his feet again, "but I thought, the R-Resident l-l-leaps, I leap too '

And here is the pendent:

In the latest cholera-scare, an old lady, the widow

of a comptroller, had been left the sole European resident
of her station, all the others having left for the hills.
The Resident, surmising inability to meet the expenses
of travel to be the reason of her staying on, offered to
convey her to a bungalow in the hills, which his own
family was then occupying. The old lady came to
thank him for the proposal, but she could not, she
said, accept it. She judged her hour had come; and
she was not afraid of death. Only one favour she would
beg from the Resident. It should be remembered that
her husband had been a comptroller, and that, as his
widow, she was in rank superior to all the European
inhabitants of the station, coming second after the Resident himself. Now her request was this: would the
Resident be so good as to leave written instructions, in
case they both should die, to the effect that her grave
should be dug next to his?

One would expect such an excess of bureaucratic
etiquette to breed dullness and constraint unspeakable.
And it certainly somewhat galls the new-comer. But
it is all an affair of custom, and after a while, these
ceremonious manners come to seem as natural and
necessary as the ordinary courtesies of life, and not a
whit more detrimental to the pleasantness of social
intercourse. Indeed, one sometimes sees positions revers-
ed, and Netherlands-Indians accusing Hollanders of
stiffness. And it must be owned that the new-comer
in Batavia-Society is struck by a certain grace and
easiness of manner that contrasts forcibly with the somewhat frigid reserve of the typical Hollander, as forcibly
as a seventeenth-century family-mansion on the Heeren-
gracht, solid, imposing and gloomy as a fortress, contrasts
with an airy Batavia-bungalow, where birds build their
nests on the capitals of the columns, and the whiteness

of the floor is tinged with slanting sunbeams and reflections of tall-leaved plants. And analogous contrasts meet one at every step. Life here has less dignity than it has in the mother-country; but it has more grace. Of its—real or seeming—necessaries, not a few are lacking. But what was that saying about the wisdom of striving for the superfluities, and caring naught for the necessaries of life? Existence in Netherland-India is based upon this principle. The superfluous is striven for— the richness and the romance of things: and everyday-life is the more acceptable for it. The comparatively poor in the colony fare better than the comparatively rich at home. They have more leisure, greater comforts and better opportunities for amusement. Hence, the prevalence of "mondain" manners.

Hospitality is another characteristic of the average Netherlands-Indian. In the mother-country a man's house is his castle; but in Java it is the castle of his guest. And his guest is practically whoever likes, a relation, a friend, a mere acquaintance, an utter stranger, his name not so much as heard of before, who comes "to bring the greetings of a friend"—as the pretty, old fashioned phrase has it: and he will meet with the most cordial of welcomes. People are not content with simply receiving a guest: they feast him. And when hospitality is offered, it is meant, not for days, but for weeks. To stay for two or three months at a friend's house is nothing out of the common; and this not for a single person merely, but for a whole family—parents, servants and all. I know I am speaking within the mark: having myself been one of nine guests, four of whom had been staying for some weeks already at a hospitable house in Batavia. And in "Java"—it is by no means rare to find an even more numerous company foregathered at the house of the Resident, who thus "does the honours" of an entire district; or at the bungalows of rich planters, jealously competing with the official for what they consider the privilege rather than the duty of hospitality. They exercise it in a truly princely way. A well-known tea-planter, some time ago, celebrating his silver wedding, commemorated the event by an entertainment, which lasted for three days, and to which a hundred and fifty guests were invited. Bamboo-huts had been erected for those who could not be accommodated in the house: barns were converted into ball-rooms and dining-halls; and the native population of half the district came and was welcomed to its share of the feast.

This of course is a signal instance, but the tendency which it illustrates is a very general one, so much so in fact, that it has influenced domestic architecture, and rendered the pavilion (the colonial epuivalent for our "spare room") as indispensable a part of the house as the bath-room and the kitchen.—Sometimes indeed the pavilion is let. But generally it remains dedicated to the uses of hospitality, and still awaits the "coming and going man," as the Dutch phrase has it. At its door welcome for ever smiles, and farewell goes out weeping.

Welcome. Farewell. Here, in Batavia, the short significant words ever and again fall upon the ear, recurrent in conversations as the deep, dominant bass-note that sends a repeated vibration through all the changes and modulatiohs of a melody; far off and distinct, as the moan of circling seas, heard in the central dells of an island where the clear-throated thrushes sing. The sensation of the temporary, the transitory and the uncertain that thrills the atmosphere of a sea-port is in the air of this seemingly-quiet inland town. It is a common saying here, that one should not make plans for more than a month beforehand. But even a month seems almost too bold a reaching into futurity, when every day is full of chances and changes, and the aspect of things alters over-night. A promotion, an attack of fever, a fluctuation in the sugar or tobacco-market, a letter from Holland—and friends are separated, homes broken up, and careers changed.

The effects of this living on short notice, if I may so call it, are perceptible in everything pertaining to colonial customs, ideas and society. I entered, the other day, one of those ancient mansions long ago degraded to offices of "the old city.". The armorial bearings of the patrician, who built it in the beginning of the preceding century, still ornament the entrance. There are stucco mouldings over the doors that lead into the great, half-dark chambers. A trace of gold and bright colours is still discernible on the blinds of the tall lattice-windows, the glass of which shines with the iridescent colours that so many days of sunshine and of rain have wrought into it; and the great staircase has an oaken balustrade richly sculptured in the style of the 17th century. The paint might be gone, the mouldings choked with dust and cobwebs, the sculptured ornaments of the balustrade defaced; but there was not a stone loose in those massive old walls nor a plank rotten in the floor. Yet, it had been abandoned. And so has the conception of life, of which it was the visible and tangible expression. Much hard-and-fastness of tradition and convention has been done away with. Where circumstances change so frequently, opinions must likewise change. As a result a certain liberality of thought has come to be a characteristic of colonial society. There is something generous and truly humane in the opinions one hears currently professed, and the courage to act up to these convictions is not wanting. But on the other hand delicacy, chivalry, and what one might call the decorum of the heart, are on the whole sadly wanting. The general tone is some-what "robustious"; this is perhaps an effect of the climate and soil. On the whole, and to give a general idea of Batavia-society, I fancy one might compare it to that of some rich provincial town. There is the same eager-ness for precedence, the same intimacy and tattle and neighbourly kindness, the same high living and plain thinking. But in the little provincial town, there is not such freedom from narrowness and prejudice, nor is there so much hard work done under such unfavourable circumstances, nor so much home-sickness and anxiety and lonely sorrow so bravely borne as in Batavia.

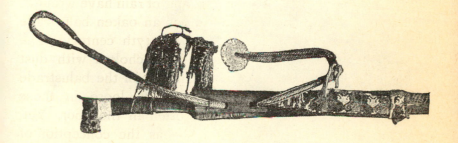

# GLIMPSES OF NATIVE LIFE

A JUST appreciation of sentiments and motives repugnant to our own is among the most difficult of intellectual feats. The Germans express their sense of this truth by a concise and vigorous, if not altogether elegant saying: "No man can get out of his own skin, and into his neighbour's." A difference of colour between the said skins, it may be added, withholds even adventurous souls from attempting the temporary transmigration. And the wisdom of nations, brown and white, sanctions this diffidence. In Java Occidentals and Orientals have been dwelling together for about three centuries. They have become conversant with each other's language, opinions and affairs; they are brought into a certain mutual dependence, and into daily and hourly contact; there is no arrogance or contempt on the one side, no abject fear or hatred on the other; no wilful prejudice, it would seem, on either. But the Hollanders do not understand the Javanese, nor do the Javanese understand the Hollanders in any true sense of the word. So that it seems the part of wisdom to acknowledge this at the outset, merely stating that the notions of nice and nasty, fair and foul, right and wrong, such as they obtain among the two nations are antagonistic. Anyway, on the part of a casual observer, such as the present writer, any further criticisms would be presumptuous and almost inevitably unjust; therefore they will be refrained from.

But, whereas I freely confess that the inner life of the Javanese has remained hidden from me, their outward existence has become familiar enough. The Javanese practically live out-of-doors. They take their bath in the river; perform their toilet under some spreading waringin-tree, hanging a mirror as big as the hand on the rugged stem; and squat down to their meal by the roadside. After nightfall, dark figures may be discerned around the stalls of fruit-vendors, fantastically lit up by the uncertain flame of an oil-wick. And in the dry season, they often sleep on the moonlit sward of some garden or on the steps of an untenanted house.

This life seems strange to us Northerners, self-constituted prisoners of roofs and walls. But we have only to look at a Malay, and the intuitive conviction flashes on us, that it is eminently right and proper for him to live in this manner. He is a creature of the field. His supple, sinewy frame, his dark skin, the far-away look in his eyes, the very shape of his feet, with the short, strong toes, well separated from one another—his whole appearance—immediately suggest a background of trees and brushwood, running water, sunlit, wind-swept spaces, and the bare brown earth. And the scenery of Java with its strange colouring, at once violent and dull, its luxuriant vegetation, and its abrupt changes in the midst of apparent monotony, lacks the final, completing touch in the absence of dusky figures moving through it. Landscape and people are each other's natural complement and explanation. Hence, the picturesque and poetic charm of the Javanese out-of-doors.

One of the most fascinating scenes is that of the bath in the river, soon after sunrise: at Batavia, I have frequently watched it from the Tanah Abang embankment The early sunlight,—a clear yellow, with a sparkle as of topazes in it—makes the dewy grass to glisten, and brightens the subdued green of the tamarind-trees along the river; between the oblique bars of shadow the brownish water gleams golden. On the bank, scores of natives are stripping for the bath. The men run down, leap into the stream, and dive under; as they come up again, their bare bodies shine like so many bronze statues. The women descend the slope with a slower step; they have pulled up their sarong over the bosom, leaving their shapely shoulders bare to the sun. At the edge of the water they pause for an instant, lifting both arms to twist their hair into a knot on the summit of the head; then entering, they bend down and wet their face and breast. Young mothers are there, leading their little ones by the hand, and coaxing them step by step further into the shallow stream. Crowds of small boys and girls have taken noisy possession of the river, plunging and splashing and calling out to each other, as they swim about, kicking up the water at every stroke of their sturdy little feet. Half hidden in a clump of tall-leaved reeds by the margin, young girls are disporting themselves, making believe to bathe, as they empty little buckets made of a palmleaf, over each other's head and shoulders, until their black hair shines, and the running water draws their garments into flowing, clinging folds, that mould their lithe little figures from bosom to ankle. Then perhaps, all of a sudden, a bamboo raft will appear round the bend of the river; or a native boat, its inmates sitting at their morning-meal under the awning; and

some friendly talk is exchanged between them and the
bathers, as the craft makes its way through the slowly-
dividing groups. One day I saw a broad, brick-laden
barge, that had thus come lumbering down the stream,
run aground on the shallows; the men jumped out, and
began pulling and shoving to get it afloat again. The

A laundry in the river.

water dripped from their tucked-up sarongs, and their
backs gleamed in the sunshine, as, almost bent double,
they urged the ponderous thing forward. But still the
bright red heap remained stationary. Suddenly, a young
boy, who had just stripped for the bath, came down the
embankment with a running leap, and giving the boat
a sudden sharp push, sent it darting forward. Then

he stood up, laughing, and shook back the shock of
black hair, which had fallen over his eyes. He looked
like a dusky young river-god, who out of his kindness
had come to assist his votaries.

The flower-market too is a scene of idyllic grace,
when, after their early bath in the river, the women
come trooping thither, and stand bargaining, their hands
full of red and pink roses, creamy jessamine, and tuberoses whiter than snow. The Javanese have a great

Native lady travelling in her litter.

love of flowers, though apparently, they take no trouble
to raise them in their gardens. In Batavia, at least, I
never saw any growing near their cottages in the kampong;
save perhaps the sturdy hibiscus in hedges, and that large
white, odoriferous convolvulus which the wind sows along
roadsides and hedgerows — the "beauty-of-the-night."
And they do not seem to care for a handful of flowers
in a vase, to brighten the semi-darkness of their little
pagar huts.

But the women are hardly ever seen without a rosebud

or tuberose-blossom twined into their hair, and the men
not unfrequently have one stuck behind the ear, or
between the folds of their head-kerchief. As for the
children, their bare brown little bodies are hung with
tandjong wreaths. The plucked-out petals of all manner
of fragrant flowers are used to scent the water which
the women pour over their long black hair, after washing
it whith a decoction of charred leaves and stalks; and
together with amber-gris and a sweet smelling root, called

A Litter.

"akhar wanggi," dried flowers are strewn between the
folds of their holiday-attire. Like all Orientals, the
Javanese are excessively fond of perfumes, which no
doubt, partially explains their profuse use of strongly-
scented flowers. But that, apart from the merely sensual
enjoyment of the smell, they prize flowers for the pleasure
afforded to the eye by their tints and shapes, is proved
by the frequency with which floral designs occur on
their clothes and ornaments. The full globes of the

lotos-buds, the disc of the unfolded flower with leaves radiating, its curiously-configurated pistil are recognized again and again on the scabbards and handles of the men's poniards and on the girdle-clasps and the large silver kabaya-brooches of the women. The fine cloth for sarongs is decorated with fanciful delineations of the flowers that blow in every field and meadow, their calixes and curly tendrils sprouting amidst figures of wide-mouthed dragons, fanged and clawed. Moreover for their hidden virtues, and the sacred meanings of which they are the symbol, flowers are by the natives associated with all the principal acts and circumstances of their lives—with joy and sorrow and ceremony, and the service of the gods. When the village folk, donning their holiday-attire, go forth to the festive planting of the rice, or the gathering, stalk by stalk, of the ripe ears, they wear wreaths of flowers twined in their hair. At the feast of his circumcision, the boy is crowned with them. They are the chief ornament of lovers on their marriage-day—gleaming in the elaborate head-dress of the bride, and dangling down as a long fringe from the groom's golden diadem; wreathing the scabbard of his poniard; and girdling his naked waist, all yellow with boreh powder. They are brought in solemn offering to the dead, when on the third, the seventh, the fortieth, the hundredth, and the thousandth day, the kinsmen visit the grave of the departed one, to pray for the welfare of his soul, and in return implore his protection and that of all the ancestors up to Adam and Eve, the parents of mankind. And lastly, flowers are thought the most acceptable offering to the gods, the ancient gods whom no violence of Buddhist or Mohammedan invader has succeeded in ousting from that safe sanctuary, the people's heart, which they share now in mutual good-will and toler-

ance, with the Toewan Allah, "besides whom there is
no God." Under some huge waringin tree, at the gate of a
town or village, an altar is erected to the tutelary genius
the "Danhjang Dessa," who has his abode in the
thick-leaved branches. And the pious people, whenever
they have any important business to transact, come to
it and bring a tribute of frankincense and flowers, to
propitiate the god, and implore his protection and
assistance, that the matter they have taken in hand
may prosper. On the way from Batavia to Meester
Cornelis, there stands such a tree by the road-side, an
immense old waringin, in itself a forest. And the rude
altar in its shade, fenced off from the public road by
a wooden railing, from sunrise to sunset is fragrant
with floral offerings.

There are several flower-markets in Batavia. But
I have taken a particular fancy to the one held at
Tanah Abang. Its site is a somewhat singularly chosen
one for the purpose, near the entrance to the cemetery,
and in the shadow of the huge old gateway, the superscription on which dedicates the place to the repose of
the dead and their pious memory. In its deep, dark
arch, as in a black frame, is set a vista of dazzling
whiteness, plastered tombstones, pillars and obelisks
huddled into irregular groups, with here and there a
figure hewn in fair white marble soaring on out-
stretched wings, and everywhere a scintillation as of
molten metal—the colourless, intolerable glare, to which
the fierce sunlight fires the corrugated zinc of the roofs
protecting the monuments.

But on the other side of the gateway there are restful
shadows and coolness. Some ancient gravestones pave
the ground, as if it were the floor of an old village-
church—bluish-grey slabs emblazoned with crests and

coats-of-arms in worn away bas-relief. Heraldic shapes are still faintly discernible on some; and long Latin epitaphs, engraved in the curving characters of the seventeenth century, may be spelt out, recording names which echo down the long corridors of time in the history of the colony; and oddly latinized, the style and title bestowed on the deceased by the Lords Seventeen, rulers of the Honourable East India Company—the Company of Far Lands, as in the olden time it was called.

Hither, before the sun is fairly risen, come a score of native flower-sellers, shivering in the morning air, who spread squares of matting on the soil, and squatting down, proceed to arrange the contents of their heaped-up baskets. The bluish-grey gravestones, with the coats-of-arms and long inscriptions, are covered with heaps of flowers: creamy Melati as delicate and sharply-defined in outline as if they had been carved out of ivory; pink and red Roses with transparent leaves, that cling to the touch; Tjempakah-telor, great smooth globes of pearly whiteness; the long calixes of the Cambodja-blossom, in which tints of yellow and pink and purple are mixed as in an evening sky; the tall sceptre of the Tuberose, flower-crowned; and "pachar china," which seems to be made out of grains of pure gold.

Some who know the tastes of the "orang blandah" have brought flowering plants to market, mostly Malmaison Roses and tiny Japanese Lilies, just dug up, the earth still clinging to their delicate roots; or they sit binding wax-white Gardenias, violet Scabiosa and leaves as downy and grey as the wings of moths, into stiff clumsy wreaths; for they have learnt that the white folks choose flowers of these dull tints to lay upon the tombs of their dead. And there is one old man, brown, shrunken and wrinkled, as if he had been made out

of the parched earth of the cemetery, who sells hand-
fuls of plucked-out petals, stirring up now and then,
with his long finger, the soft, fragrant heap in his
basket—thousands of brilliantly-coloured leaflets.

About seven o'clock the customers, almost exclusively
women, arrive, fresh from their bath in the neighbouring river. They form picturesque groups on the
sunny road, those slender figures in their brigh-hued
garments, pink, and red, and green, their round brown
faces and black hair still wet and shining, framed in
the yellow aureole of the payong * which they hold
spread out behind their head. And the quiet spot in
the shadow of the cemetery-gate is alive with their
high-pitched twittering voices, as they go about from
one flower-seller to another, bargaining for Jessamines,
Orange-blossoms, and tiny pink Roses, which, with deft
fingers, they twist into the glossy coil of their "kondeh."

Javanese women are most pardonably pround of their
hair. It is somewhat coarse, but very long and thick
and of a brilliant black, with bluish gleams in it; and
it prettily frames their broad forehead with regular,
well-defined curves and points. They take great care
of it too, favourably contrasting, in this respect with
European women of the lower classes, though some of
their methods, it must be owned, are repugnant to
European notions of decency. As they bathe and sleep,
and eat in public, so in public, they cleanse each
other's hair. A woman will squat down in some shady
spot by the roadside, and shaking loose her coiled-up
hair, submit to the manipulations of a friend, who parts
the strands with her spread-out fingers, and removes . . . .
superfluities, with quick monkey-like gestures. What
would you have? "The country's manner, the country's

---

* The payong is an umbrella, quite flat when spread out, of yellow oiled paper.

honour," as the Dutch proverb hath it. This particular way of cleansing the hair is a national institution among the Javanese. And as such it is celebrated in the legends of the race, and in the tales of the olden time, which are still repeated of an evening among friends.

The scholar of the party, by the light of an oil-wick, reads from a greasy manuscript which he has hired

Street-Dancers.

for the evening at the price of one "pitji." * It is the story of the beautiful beggarmaid, who wanders from village. She does not know her own name or who were her parents, having, in infancy, been stolen by robbers. One day she comes begging to the gates of the palace. The Rajah orders the guards to admit the suppliant, and his Raden-Ajoe † causes a repast to be

* About twopence. † Chief wife.

prepared for her. They are kind towards those in
affliction, having known great sorrow themselves: for
their only child, a daughter, mysteriously disappeared
years and years ago; and now they are old and child-
less. The Rajah, gazing upon the stranger, frequently
sighs: his daughter would have grown up to be a
maiden as fair, if she had lived. And the Raden-
Ajoe, taking her by the hand, bids her sit down and
unloose those glossy locks, worthy to be wreathed with

Musicians.

the fragrant blossom of the asana. She herself will
cleanse them. Then, as she parts the long braids, ah!
there upon the crown, behold the cicatrice which her
little daughter had! The long-lost one is found again

In Javanese fairy-tales the long locks of nymphs and
goddesses are treasured as talismans by the hero who
has been fortunate enough to obtain one. There is
great virtue for instance, in the long hair of the Pontianak, the cruel sprite that haunts the waringin tree.

Clasp for fastening a kabaya in front.

Have you never seen her glide by, white in the silver moonlight? Have you never heard her laugh, loud and long, when all was still? She is the soul of a dead virgin, whom no lover ever kissed. And now she

The native cithara and violin.

cannot rest, because she never knew love; and she would fain win it yet; though not in kindness now, but in spite and deadly malice. She sits in the branches of trees, softly singing to herself as she combs her long hair. And when a young man, hearing her song pauses to listen, she meets him in the semblance of a maid fairer than the bride of the Love-god, and raises soft eyes to him and smiling lips. But, when he would embrace her, he feels the gaping wound in her back, which she had concealed under her long hair. And as he stands speechless with horror, she breaks away from him with a long loud laugh, and cries: "Thou

A Native Restaurant in its most compendious shape.

hast kissed the Pontianak, thou must die!" And ere the moon is full again, his kinsmen will have brought flowers to his grave. But if he be quick-witted and courageous, he will seize the evil spirit by her flying locks; and if he succeeds but in plucking out one single hair, he will not die, but live to a great age, rich, honoured and happy, the husband of a Rajah's daughter and the father of Princes.

Some men are fortunate, however, from their birth, and do not need the Pontianak's long hair; that is because their own grows in a peculiar manner, from two circular spots near the crown. To the owner of such a "double crown," nothing adverse can ever happen. All his wishes will be fulfilled, and he will prosper in whatever matter he sets his hand to.

Again it is not men alone who are thus visibly marked by fate. In the crinklings of the hair on a horse's neck, the wise read plain signs of good or bad fortune, by which it is made manifest whether the horse will be lucky and carry his rider to honour and happiness, or unlucky and maim or even kill him. That is the great point about a horse: the way in which the hair on his neck grows. If therefore you should find the auspicious sign on him, buy the animal, whatever may be the price and however old, ugly or weak he may seem to the ignorant. But if you find the sign of ill-luck, send him away at once, and cause the marks of his hoofs to be carefully obliterated from the path that leads to your door; for if you neglect this precaution, great disaster may be brought upon you and all your house. Reflect upon this, and the true significance of the history of Damocles will be revealed to you. In truth, all fortune, good or bad, hangs by a single hair.

After the bath, the Javanese proceeds to take his morning meal; and this again is a public performance. The noon repast—the only solid one in the day—is prepared and eaten at home. But for the morning and evening meals, the open air and the cuisine of the warong are preferred. The warong is the native restaurant. There are many kinds and varieties of it: from its most simple and compendious shape—two wooden cases, the one containing food, prepared and raw, the

other, a chafing-dish full of live coals, and a supply
of crockery—to its fully-developed form, the atap-
covered hut. There a dozen and more customers hold
their symposia presided over by the owner, who sits
cross-legged on the counter amid heaps of fruit, vege-

For the morning and evening meal he prefers the open air and the cuisine of the warong.

tables and confectionery. All manner of men meet
here: drivers of sadoos or hack-carriages, small merchants,
artizans, Government clerks, policemen, water-carriers,
servants, hadjis, * not to mention the "corresponding"
womankind. They talk, they talk! and they laugh!
The affairs of all Batavia are discussed here—matters

* Title given to those who have performed the pilgrimage to Mecca.

of business, intrigue, love, money, office, everything, material to make a Javanese Decamerone of, if a Boccaccio would but come and put it into shape. There are several of these warongs about Tanah-Abang and the Koningsplein, and of course in the native quarters. But the smaller, portable ones are found everywhere: by the river-side, at the railway stations, at the sadoo-stands, along the canals, at the corners of the streets; and they seem to do a thriving business.

Each of these itinerant cooks has his own place on the pavement or in the avenue, recognised as such by the tacit consent of the others. Hither he comes trudging in the early morning, carefully balancing his cases at the end of the long bamboo yoke, so as not to break any of the dozens of cups, glasses, and bottles on his tray; then, having disposed his commodities in the most appetizing manner, he stirs up the charcoal in the chafing-dish, and begins culinary operations. One of these is the preparation of the coffee, which consists of pouring boiling water upon the leaves, instead of the berries of the coffee-tree, after the manner of some Arab tribes. Sometimes however, the berries also are used, and the infusion is sweetened with lumps of the dark-brown, faintly flavoured sugar that is won from the areng-palm. Then the rice—the principal dish of this, as of any other meal—is boiled in a conical bag of plaited palm fibre; and, when ready, is made up into heaped-up portions, with perhaps, a bit of dried fish and some shreds of scarlet lombok * stuck on the top. This is for the solid part of the repast; the dessert is next thought of. It is ready in the portable cupboard—the thrifty wife of the vendor having risen long before dawn to prepare it—and is now set

* The seed-capsules of the red pepper-plant.

forth, on strips of torn-up banana-leaf, as on plates
and saucers; green and withe balls of rice-meal, powdered
over with rasped cocoa-nut, orange cakes of Indian
corn, shaking pink jellies, and slices of some tough
dark-brown stuff. The cool fresh green of the banana-
leaf makes the prettiest contrast imaginable to all these
colours, its silky surface and faint fragrance giving at
the same time, an impression of dainty cleanliness such
as could never be achieved by even the most spotless
linen and china of a European dining-table.

The Javanese are very frugal eaters. A handful of
rice with a pinch of salt, and perhaps a small dried
fish being sufficient for a day's ration. Of course, we
Europeans confessedly eat too much. But how grossly
we over-eat ourselves, can only be realized on seeing
a Javanese subsisting on about a tenth part of our
own daily allowance, and doing hard work on that—
labouring in the field, travelling on foot for days together, and carrying heavy loads without apparent
over-exertion.

However, though so abstemious in the matter of
solid food, they are excessively fond of sweetmeats. I
have often watched a party of grown men and women,
seated on the low bench in front of a warong, and
eating kwee-kwee * with perfectly childish relish, or
bending over a stall, gravely comparing the respective
charms of white, pink, and yellow cakes; hesitating,
consulting the confectioner, and at last solving the
difficulty by eating a little of everything. Whatever
ready money they may chance to have, is spent either
on personal adornment or on sweetmeats; and on festive
occasions, they will pawn their furniture rather than
deny themselves the enjoyment of more cakes, jellies,

* Malay for "cakes."

fruit and syrups than they can partake of without making themselves sick and sorry.

Nor do they show more discretion in the matter of the dieting of their children. Though left, in almost all other respects, to chance and the guidance of its

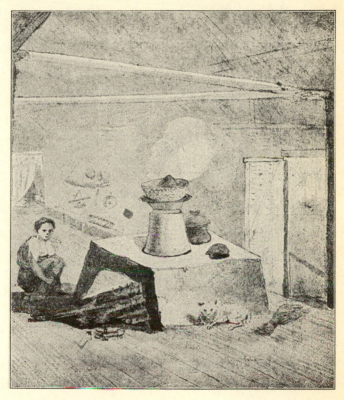

A kitchen.

own instincts, a native child is not trusted to eat alone. The mother's idea seems to be, that, if left to itself, her child would never eat at all, and that it is her plain duty to correct this mistake in nature's plan. Wherefore, having prepared a mess of rice and banana,

she lays the little thing flat on its back, upon her
knees, takes some of the food between the tips of her
fingers, kneading it into a little lump, and pushes this
into the baby's mouth, cramming it down the throat
with her thumb, when the baby, willy nilly, must
swallow it. Thus she goes on, the baby alternately
screaming and choking, until she judges it has had
enough— is full to the brim, so to speak, and incapable
of holding another grain of rice. Then she will set

A native restaurant in its simplest and most compendious shape

it on its feet again, dry the tears off its round cheeks,
and rock it to sleep against her breast, closefolded in
the long "slendang."

A similar principle obtains in education. To watch
the native schoolmaster drilling the Koran into his
pupils, is to be reminded of the rice-balls and the maternal
thumb. I witnessed the scene, the other day, at a little
school—if a framework of four bamboo-posts and an
"atap" roof deserves that name—in a native "kampong"

at Meester Cornelis. * I had come upon this school
quite accidentally, in the course of a ramble along the
river-side. As I was making my may through a plantation
of slim young trees, all festooned with dangling lianas,
I had been conscious for some minutes of a droning and
buzzing sound somewhere near me, and fancied it to be
the humming of bees, hovering over the lantana-blossoms
that covered the steep bank of the river with flames of
red and orange, and filled the air with their pungent
scent. But suddenly, I caught the word „Allah", and
the next moment, I was standing in an open space in
the midst of some ten or twelve bamboo huts. One
of these, evidently, was a school; and the droning noise
I had heard proceeded from an old spectacled schoolmaster, who was reading aloud—or rather chanting—
from a book held in his hand. A little boy stood in
front of him, listening very attentively, and every time
the old schoolmaster had completed a phrase, the child
repeated it in exactly the same sing-song, closing his
eyes the while, and rocking his little body to and fro.
After he had finished, another came up; there were some
twelve or thirteen seated on a sort of bench, awaiting
their turn; and all of them went through the same
course of listening and repeating, the master, now and
then, correcting the intonation of some phrase. It was
the Koran which they were thus reciting in the Arabic
language. In all probability, the master did not understand a single word of Arabic; assuredly none of the
boys did. But what of that? They know it by heart,
from its very first word to its very last. They learn to
mis-pronounce the Confession of the Unity of God; and
they are taught to consider themselves Mohammedans.
That is enough.

* A suburb of Batavia.

After the early morning meal, the Javanese begin the business of the day. In towns, where they are debarred their natural occupation, agriculture, and where, moreover, the Chinese artisans and shopkeepers have almost entirely ousted them from trade and commerce, the majority of the natives, men and women, are employed as domestic servants in the houses of European residents. Hence, but little is seen of them during the greater part

Native restaurant.

of the day. Towards four o'clock, they reappear, and again repair to the kali or the canal for a plunge into the tepid water. Cigarettes are lit, sirih-leaves cut up and neatly rolled into a quid and some friendly conversation is indulged in. In fine weather games are played.

The behaviour of Javanese at play is one of the things which strike most strongly upon the Northerner's observation. There is nothing here of that vociferous

Breakfast in the open air.

enthusiasm which characterises our young barbarians at play—no shouts of exultation or defiance, no applause, no derision, no cries, no quarrelling or noisy contest. From beginning to end of the game, a sedate silence prevails. This is not, as might be imagined, due to apathy and indifference—the Javanese are keen sportsmen, and often stake comparatively important sums on the issue of a game—but the effect of an etiquette which condemns demonstrativeness as vulgar. Outward placidity must be maintained, whatever the stress of the emotions, and whether circumstances be important or trivial. Hence the apparent calm of Javanese at play, even when engaged in games that most excite their naturally fierce passions of ambition and envy. The winner does not seem elated, the loser is not spiteful. They are in the full sense of the word "beaux joueurs."

During the East monsoon, when high south-easterly winds may be counted upon, flying kites is a favorite game; and not only with boys, but with grown men. Groups of them may often be seen in the squares and parks of Batavia or in the fields near the town, floating large kites, shaped like birds and winged dragons, which in ascending, emit a whistling sound, clear and plaintive as that of a wind-harp. They sometimes remain soaring for days together, and strains of that aerial music, attuned in sad "minore," float out upon every passing breath of air. Passers-by in the street look up, shading their eyes from the sun, at the bright things soaring and singing in the sky, and dispute much about the melodious merits of each.

The paper singing-birds, called "swangan," are very popular with the masses. But the true amateurs of the sport prefer another kind: the "palembang" and "koenchier" kites, which do not sing but fight, or at least, in skilful hands, can be made to fight. These are made of Chinese paper, and decorated with the image of some god or hero of Javanese mythology. The cord twisted out of strong rameh fibre is coated with a paste of pounded glass or earthenware, mixed with starch. This renders it strong and cutting as steel wire. The aim of each player is to make the cord of his kite, when up in the air, cross his opponent's cord, and then, with a swift downward pull, cut it in two: a manœuvre which requires considerable dexterity. The game is played according to strict rules and with some degree of ceremony and etiquette, as prescribed by the "adat"—the immemorial law of courtesy, which in Java regulates all things, from matters of life and death down to the arrangement of a girl's scarf and the games which children play. When all the kites are well up in the air, tugging on the strained cords, each player chooses his antagonist. He advances to within a few paces, makes his kite approach the other's, all but touch it, swerve and come back; having thus preferred his challenge, he retires to the place first occupied. Thither presently his opponent follows him, and by the exact repetition of his manœuvre, signifies his acceptance of the combat, retiring afterwards in the same stately manner. Then the contest begins. The agile figures of the players dart hither and thither, fitfully, with swift impulse and sudden pause, and abrupt swerve, bending this way and that, swaying with head thrown back and right arm flung up along the straining cord. The groups of spectators, standing well aside so as not to interfere with the movements of the players, gaze upward with bated breath. And aloft, sparkling with purple and gold, their long streamers spread out upon the wind, the two kites soar and swoop, swerve, plunge a second time, slowly swim upwards again, glide a little further, and hang motionless. The thin cords are all but invisible; the fantastic shapes high in the air seem animated with a life of their own, wilful, untiring, eager to pursue, and swift to escape, full of feints and ruses. Suddenly, as one again plunges, the other, tranquilly sailing aloft, trembles, staggers, tumbles over, and leaping up, scuds down the wind and is gone. The severed length of cord comes down with a thud, and as the unlucky owner darts away after the fugitive, in the forlorn hope of finding it hanging somewhere in the branches of a tree, the victor lets his kite re-ascend and triumphantly hover aloft, straining against the wind, and tugging upon the strong shiny cord that has come off scathless from the encounter.

The aboriginal craving for battle and mastery, which, philosophers tell us, is at the bottom of all our games, is even more strongly developed in the Javanese than in the Caucasian. But the race is not an athletic one; immemorial traditions of decorum condemn hurry and violence of movement; and active games, such as this of flying kites, are the exception. Even at play the Javanese loves repose; and when gratifying his combative instincts, he is mostly content to fight by proxy.

Cocks and crickets are the chosen deputies of the town-folk in this matter; and Javanese sportsmen are as enthusiastic about them as Spaniards about a toreador, and Englishmen about a prize-fighter.

The Government forbids the cock- and cricket-fights on account of the gambling to which they invariably give rise. But the police are not omniscient or ubiquitous. Where there is a will, there is a way; and in hidden corners, cocks continue to hack, and crickets to bite and kick each other to the greater amusement of native sporting circles.

On the training of a game-cock, his owner spends much time, care and forethought. The bird's diet is regulated to a nicety: so much boiled rice per diem, so much water, so much meat, hashed fine and mixed with medicinal herbs. Once a week a bath is given him, after which he is taken in his coop to a sunny place to dry; and he is subjected to a regular course

Here they are: without plaything naked, and supremely happy.

of massage at the hands of his trainer, who, taking the bird into his lap, with careful finger and thumb, "pichits" or shampoos the muscles of neck, wings and legs, to make them supple and strong. Connoisseurs arrive from compound and "kampongs" to exchange criticisms. The age, strength and agility of rival birds are discussed at length and finally, when there is a sufficient number in good condition, a match is arranged.

The amateurs arrive at the spot, each carrying his

bird cooped up in a cage of banana-leaves, through opposite openings in which the head, shorn of its comb, and the tail protrude. A ring is formed, every one squatting down, with his cage in front of him; and the birds are taken out and passed round for general

A Chinese carpenter.

inspection. After careful comparison and deliberation, two of approximately equal strength are selected as antagonists, and the umpire, whose office it is to arm the birds with the trenchant steel spurs, further equalizes chances by attaching the weapons of the weaker party to the spot where they will prove most effective: high up the leg. The owners then take up each his own bird, allow the two to peck at each other once or twice, put them down upon the ground again, and at the signal given by the umpire, let go. The cocks fight furiously. Generally one of the two is killed; and almost inevitably, both are cruelly injured by the long, two-edged knives attached to their legs in place of the cut-off spurs.

Cricket-fights do not seem quite as brutal: the natural weapons of the little combatants, at least, are not artificially added to; and victory, it appears, is as often achieved by courage and skill as by mere force. It is said that even more patience is required to train a game-cock; and the process certainly seems elaborate.

First, there is the catching of the "changkrik." For this the amateur goes after nightfall to some solitary spot out in the fields or woods—preferably near the grave of some Moslem saint or royal hero, or in the shadow of some sacred tree; the "changkriks" caught in these consecrated places being considered much superior to those of the ditch and garden as participating in the virtue of their habitat. Here then, the amateur builds some stones into a loose heap, hiding in the midst of it a decoy "changkrik" in a little bamboo cage and retreats. When, a little before dawn, he again approaches the spot, treading cautiously and shading the light of his little lantern, he is sure to surprise quite a company of crickets gathered around the mound and crouching under the stones, whither they have been lured by the shrill song of the captive insect; and if he is adroit, he may catch a score at a time. Only the finest and strongest of these he retains; and straightway the work of education is begun.

This is not easy; for the cricket is among the most

liberty-loving of animals, and at first, utterly refuses to be tamed. Unless the bamboo of which his little cage is made, be very hard and close-grained, he manages to gnaw his way through it, and when baulked in this attempt, tries to shatter the walls of his prison by battering them with his horny head, never ceasing until he has killed or, at any rate, stunned himself. In order to tame him, his trainer throws the "changkrik" into a basin full of water, and there lets him struggle and kick until he is half-drowned and quite senseless; then fishing out the little inert body, he puts it in the palm of his hand, and with a tiny piece of cotton-wool fastened to a "lidi" *, begins to stroke and rub it, in a kind of lilliputian massage. Then pulling out a long lank hair from the shock hidden under his "kain kapala" †, he delicately ties it round one of the cricket's hind legs, and hangs him to a nail in some cool draughty place, where the air may revive him. After a couple of hours perhaps, the tiny creature, dangling by one leg, begins to stir. It is then taken down, warmed in the hollow of the hand, encouraged to stand upon its legs, and crawl a little way, and finally replaced in its bamboo cage. It does not again try to escape.

When it has thus been brought to the proper frame of mind, its real education begins. With a very fine brush made of grass-blossoms the trainer tickles its head, side and back; a mettlesome individual immediately begins to "crick" angrily, and to snap at the teasing brush. After some time he flies at the brush as soon as he sees it, hanging on to it with his strong jaws, as to a living thing. This shows he is in good

* Lidi: — Fibre from the stalk of the palm leaf.
† Kain Kapala: — Head-kerchief.

condition for fighting. He is now, for some days, fed upon rice sprinkled with cayenne-pepper, to "prick him in his courage"; and then taken to the arena. His antagonist is there, in his narrow bamboo-cage, quivering with impatience under the touch of his trainer's brush of grass-blossoms; the cages are placed over against one another; and as soon as they are opened,

Scene in a Wayang-Wong place.

the two "changkriks" rush at each other. The one who is first thrown or who turns tail and flies, is beaten; and great is the glory of the victor. The Javanese often stake comparatively important sums on fighting crickets. And there is always a chance that the quarrel of the tiny champions may be fought out by their owners.

*   *   *

To all other pleasures, the Javanese prefers that of witnessing a performance of the wayang, the native theatre. He is an artist at heart, loving sweet sounds, graceful movements, and harmonies of bright colour; and all these he may enjoy at the wayang, where, in the pauses of the drama, ballads are sung to the tinkling accompaniment of the "gamellan," and splendidly-arrayed dancers put forth "the charm of woven paces

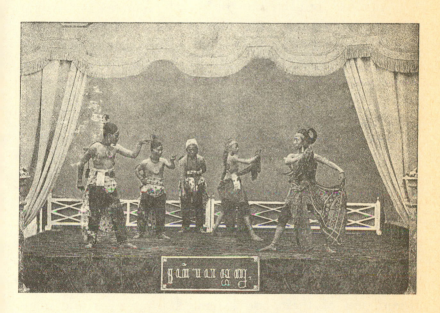

The Regent of Malang's Wayang-Wong.

and of waving hands." There are several kinds of "wayang," each having its own range of subjects and style of acting; the most ancient as well as the most popular however, is the "wayang poerwa," the miniature stage on which the lives and adventures of Hindoo-heroes, queens, and saints are acted over again by puppets of gilt and painted leather, moving in the hands of the "dalang," who recites the drama.

The "wayang poerwa" is best described as a combina-
tion of a "Punch-and-Judy" show and a kind of "Chinese
shadows"; and—as with the famed shield which was
silver on one side and gold on the other—its appearance
depends upon the stand-point of the spectator. A puppet-
show to those in front of the screen, where the gaudily-
painted figures are fixed in a piece of banana-stem, it
is a Chinese lantern to those on the other side, who see
the shadows projected on the luminous canvas. According
to ancient custom, the men sit in front and see the
puppets; the women have their place behind the screen,
and look on at the play of the shadows. In fully-
equipped wayangs, as many as two hundred of these
puppets are found, each with its own particular type
and garb, characteristic of the person represented.

Certain conventional features however, are repeated
throughout as symbols of their moral disposition. Long
thin noses continuing the line of the sloping forehead,
narrow, slanting eyes and delicate mouths, firmly shut,
indicate wisdom and a gentle disposition; a bulging
forehead, short thick nose, round eyes and gaping mouth,
indicate lawlessness and violence. No difference is made
between the portraitures of gods and those of mortals;
but the Titans are distinguished by the size and un-
wieldiness of their body, their staring eyes and huge
teeth, sometimes resembling tusks. The bodies and faces
are indifferently black, blue, white, flesh-coloured or
gilt; the colour of the face, moreover, often being a
different one from that of the rest of the person. And
all the figures are taken in profile.

The stage on which these puppets are shown consists
of an upright screen of white sarong-cloth. A lamp
hangs from the top; at the bottom it has a transverse
piece of banana-stem, into the soft substance of which

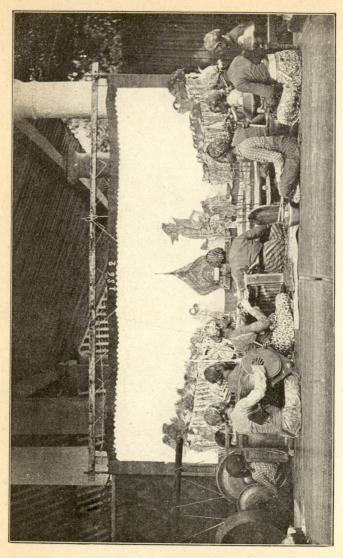

The miniature stage on which the lives and adventures of Hindoo heroes, queens and saints are acted over again by puppets of gilt and painted leather.

The native orchestra which accompanies every representation of the wayang.

the puppets may easily be fixed by means of the long sharp point in which their supports terminate. The centre of the screen is occupied by the "gunungan," the conventionalized representation of a wooded hill, which symbolizes the idea of locality in general, and stands for a town, a palace, a lake, a well, the gate of Heaven, the stronghold of the Titans, in short for any and every place mentioned in the course of the drama. Among the further accessories of the wayang are a set of miniature weapons, shields, swords, spears, javelins and "krisses," exactly copied after those now or formerly in use among Javanese, and often of the most exquisite workmanship, destined to be handled by the gods and the heroes to whose hands they are very ingeniously adapted. Nor should such items as horses and chariots be forgotten. To manœuvre this lilliputian company of puppets is the difficult task of the "dalang."

In continuance of the Punch-and-Judy comparison, the "dalang" should be called the "showman" of the wayang. But he is a showman on a grand scale. Not only does he make his puppets act their parts of deities, heroes, and highborn beauties according to the strict canons of Javanese dramatic art, observant at the same time of the exigencies of courtly etiquette, but he must know by heart the whole of those endless epics, the recitation of which occupies several nights; sometimes he himself dramatizes some popular myth or legend; and he must always be ready at a moment's notice to imagine new and striking episodes, adapt a scene from another play to the one he is performing, and improvise dialogues in keeping with the character of the dramatis personæ. He should have an ear for music and a good voice, and possess some knowledge of Kawi * to give at all well

* Ancient Javanese.

the songs written in that ancient tongue, which announce the arrival of the principal characters on the stage. Moreover he conducts the "gamellan," the native orchestra which accompanies every representation of the wayang; and finally he orders the symbolical dance, which gorgeously-attired "talèdèks" execute in the pauses of the drama. Manager, actor, musician, singer, reciter, improvisator, and all but playwright, he is in himself a pleiad of artists.

But the "dalang's" reward is proportionate to those exertions. He and his art are alike held in almost superstitious respect. No one dreams of criticizing his performances. If he wishes to travel, not a town or hamlet but will give him an enthusiastic welcome. And at home he enjoys that princely prerogative, immunity from taxes, his fellow-citizens discharging his obligations in requital of the pleasure he procures them by his wayang-performances. If nothing else were known about them, this one trait, it seems to me, would be sufficient to prove the Javanese to be a people capable of true enthusiasm, and a generous conception of life. There is something Greek in this notion, that holds the artist acquitted of all other duties towards the community, since he fulfils the supreme one of giving joy.

At the same time that it is the chief national amusement, the wayang-show is, in a sense, a religious act, performed in honour of the deity, and to invoke the blessing of the gods and the favour of the "danhjang dessa" and all other good spirits upon the giver of the entertainment. The baleful influence of the Evil Eye also, is averted by nothing so surely as by a wayang-performance, wherefore no enterprise of any importance should be entered upon without one of these miniature dramatical representations being given. Domestic feasts

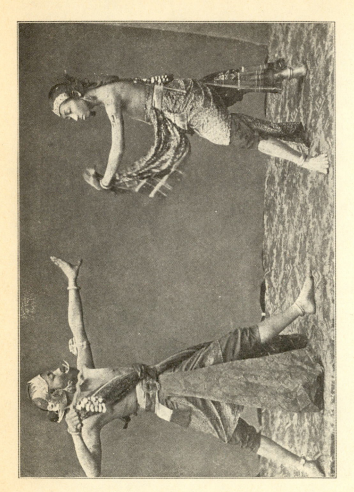

Wayang-Wong Players missing a Fight.

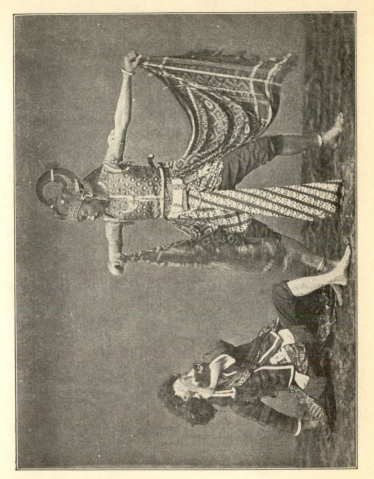

Wayang-Wong Scene.

such as are held at the birth of a child, or at his circumcision, seldom lack this additional grace. And a marriage at which Brahma, Indra, and above all Ardjuna, the beloved of women, had not been present in effigy, would be considered ill-omened from the beginning.

As soon as it becomes known that some well-known "dalang" will hold a wayang-performance at such and such a house, * the village-folk from miles around come trooping toward the spot, trudging for hours or even days, along the sun-scorched, dust-choked highroads, an enormous, mushroom-shaped that on their head, and a handful of boiled rice, neatly folded in a green leaf, tucked into their girdle. At one of the numerous warongs or shops temporarily erected near the spot, where the wayang is to be performed, they buy some bananas and a cup of hot water, flavoured perhaps with green leaves of the coffee-plant, and sweetened with the aromatic areng-sugar. And provided with these simple refreshments, they squat down upon the ground—the men on that side of the wayang-screen where they will see the puppets, the women on the other where the shadows are seen—and prepare to restfully enjoy the drama.

Already the last streaks of crimson and gold-shot opal have faded in the western skies, and the grey of dusk begins to deepen into nocturnal blackness. The evening breeze is astir in the tall tree-tops, waking a drowsy bird here and there among the branches; it chirps sleepily and is still again. Aloft a single star is seen limpid and tremulous, like a dewdrop about to fall. And the garrulous groups around the wayang-screen gradually cease their talk.

Now the "dalang" rising, disposes, on an improvised

* The wayang-screen is erected in the open air, in front of the house.

altar, the sacrificial gifts—fruit, and yellow rice, and
flowers, and lights the frankincense that keeps off evil
spirits. Then, as the column of odoriferous smoke ascends,
sways and disperses through the thin, cool air, a volley
of thunderous sound bursts from the "gamellan," and
the dancers appear.

Slowly they advance, in hand-linked couples, gliding
rather than walking with so gentle a motion, that it
never stirs the folds of their trailing robes, gathered
at the waist by a silver clasp. Their bare shoulders,
anointed with boreh, * gleam duskily above the purple
slendang that drapes the bosom. Their soft round faces
are set in a multi-coloured coruscation of jewellery, a
play of green and blue and ruby-red sparks, that chase
each other along the coiled strands of the necklace and
the trembling ear-pendants, and shine with a steadier
light in the richly chased tiara. A broad silver band,
elaborately ornamented, clasps the upper arm; a narrower
bracelet encircles the wrist; the fingers are a-glitter
with rings.

Arrived in front of the wayang-screen they pause,
with the tips of their fingers take hold of the long
embroidered scarfs and stand expectant of the music
that is to accompany their dancing. The "gamellan"
intones a plaintive melody: a medley of tinkling, and
fluting, and bell-like sounds, scanded by the long-drawn
notes of the "rebab," the Persian viol. Following the
impulse of its rhythm, the dancers raise their hands
making the scarf to float along the extended arm and
waving about the glittering silk they drape themselves
in its folds as in a veil. Then, standing with feet turned
slightly inwards, and motionless, they begin to turn and
twist the body, bending this way and that way with

* A fragrant yellow unguent.

the swaying movement of slim young trees that bow
beneath the passing breeze, tossing their branches. And
with arms extended and hands spread out, they mime
a ballad, which some of their companions are singing,

Scene from a Wayang-Wong-play.

the prologue to the play. This may be a fragment of
that ancient Hindoo-poem, the Maha-Bharata; or a myth
of which Brahma, Vishnu and Shiwa are the heroes,
such as there are recorded in the Manik Maja; or again,

some episode of the Ramayana; the "wayang poerwa" being dedicated to the representation of these three epics. A favourite subject, popular with the men on account of the many battles occurring in the course of the drama, and with the women because Ardjuna, the gentle hero, has the leading part, is the rebellion and defeat of the Titans.

In the first scene the gods appear on either hand of the "gunungan"; Indra and Brahma hold anxious counsel as to what course of action shall be pursued, now that the audacious Titans have dared to march against the abode of the gods; for already their armies occupy the four quarters of Heaven, and the insolent Raksasa, their king and general, fears not the arms of the gods, their deadly swords and intolerable lances, for his huge body—all but one hidden spot—is invulnerable. And none may conquer him, except a mortal hero, pure of all passion and sin. Sorrowfully Brahma lifts his hands. "Such a one exists not." But Indra bethinks him of Ardjuna, the gentle prince, who, having utterly forsworn the glories of warfare, the pride of worldly rank and station, and the love of women, has retired to a cavern on Mount Indra Kila; and under the name of Sang Parta—assumed instead of the kingly one of Ardjuna—leads a life of prayer and penitence, mortifying his flesh, and still keeping his constant thought fixed on Shiwa, the giver of Victory. "Maybe Sang Parta is the hero destined to overcome Niwâtakawaka."

And the other gods, divided between hope and fear, answer: "Let us put his virtue to the test, that we may know surely." Among the heavenly nymphs, "the widadari," there are seven, the fairest of all famous for many victories over saintly priests and anchorites, whom, by a smile, they caused to break the vows they had vowed, and forsake the god to whom they had

"Topeng" played by masked actors.

"Topeng" actors.

dedicated themselves. These now are sent to tempt Ardjuna. If he withstands them, he will be indeed victor of the god of Love.

The nymphs descend on Mount Indra Kila. "The wild kine and the deer of the mountain raise their head to gaze after them as they frolic over the dew-lit grass. The cinnamon trees put forth young shoots, less red than the maidens' lips. And the boulders, strewn around Sang

Slowly they advance gliding rather than walking.

Parta's cavern, glisten to welcome them, as one by one they pass the dark entrance." But the hermit, absorbed in pious contemplations, never turns his averted head, never looks upon the lovely ones, nor deigns to listen to their wooing songs. And those seven fair queens are fain to depart, hiding their face, smarting with the pain of unrequited love.

But the gods, beholding them come back thus shame-faced and sad, rejoice exceedingly.

Now, to put Sang Parta's courage to the test, Shiwa,

the terrible one, assumes mortal shape; and descending on Indra Kila, defies the hermit. They fight, and Sang Parta is victor. Then Shiwa, revealing himself, praises the anchorite for his piety and his valour; and for a reward, bestows upon him his own never-failing spear. After which he returns to the council of the gods, bidding them be of good cheer, for now it cannot be doubted any longer that Sang Parta is the hero destined to conquer the unconquerable Raksasa.

Street-dancers.

He is now summoned to the presence of the gods, and receives their command to go forth and slay the Raksasa. A goddess arms him; and a nymph whispers into his ear the secret on which the Titan's life depends: his vulnerable spot is the tip of his tongue. Sang Parta now resumes his real name; and as Ardjuna goes to seek Niwatakawata. After many wanderings and perilous adventures, in which Shiwa's miraculous spear stands him in good stead, he finally meets his

A Nipah Palm.

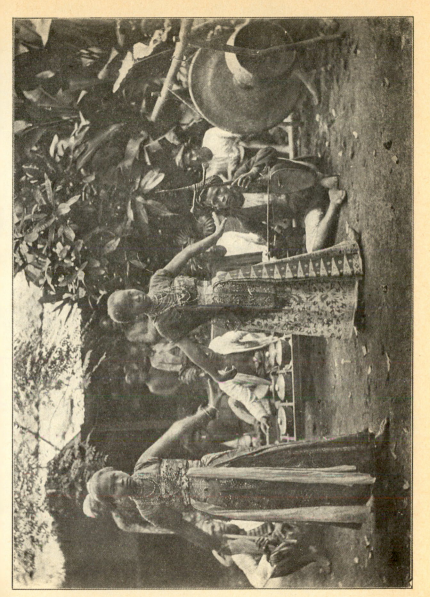

The dancers stand listening for the music.

destined antagonist, and defies him to single combat. For a long time they fight, each in turn seeming victor and vanquished, until at last, Ardjuna, feigning to have received a deadly thrust, sinks down. Then, as the Raksasa, skipping about in insolent joy, shouts out a defiance to the gods, Ardjuna hurls his spear at the monster's wide-opened mouth and pierces his tongue; and the blasphemer drops down dead. The other Titans

A Wayang representation.

seeing their king fallen, fly, and the gods are saved. But Ardjuna is rewarded for his exploits, the grateful gods bestowing upon him seven surpassingly fair "widadari," a kingdom, and the power of working miracles.

This drama, called Ardjuna's marriage-feast, is a comparatively short one, which may be performed in the course of one night. The majority of wayang-plays however, require three or four nights, or even a whole week, for an adequate representation; and there are some which last for a fortnight. They consist of fourteen, fifteen, or even more acts. The number of dramatis personæ is practically unlimited; new heroes and heroines constantly appear upon the scene; and to render confusion still worse confounded, they again and again change their names. Time is annihilated, the babe, whose miraculous birth is represented in the

A Wayang representation.

beginning of an act, having arrived at man's estate before the end of it, and one generation succeeding another in the course of the play. Generally too, no trace of any regular plan is discoverable. Incident follows incident, and intrigue disconnected intrigue; and at every turn, fresh dramatic elements are introduced. So that, as the drama ceases—for it cannot in any proper sense be said to finish—characters whose very names have not been mentioned before, are making love, waging war, and holding desultory counsel about events absolutely irrelevant and between which and those represented in the beginning of the drama, it is all but impossible to find the slightest connection.

Wayang dancers.

To a Javanese, these endless plays hardly seem long enough. He never wearies of the innumerable adventures of these innumerable heroes, titans, queens and gods, though he has seen them represented ever since he was a child, and probably knows them by heart,

almost as well as the "dalang" himself. He has no
prejudice in favour of any regular intrigue with beginning, catastrophe and end. And as for improba-
bilities, many strange things happen, day by day.
And as for time, was not the Prophet carried
up to Heaven to sojourn among the blessed for a
thousand years, whence returning to Mecca, and entering his chamber, he found the pitcher, which he had
upset in his heavenward flight, not yet emptied of its
contents? Such considerations cannot spoil his enjoyment of the wayang. Night after night the Javanese
sit, listening to the grandiloquent speeches of the heroes
and their courting of queens and nymphs, discussing
their opinions and principles, moral and otherwise; and
amid bursts of laughter, applauding any witticism, with
which the "dalang" may enliven his somewhat monotonous text. And as at last, they regretfully rise in
the reddening dawn that causes the wayang-lights to
pale, visions of that heroic and beautiful world accompany them on their homeward way. The maidens would
hardly be amazed to behold Ardjuna slumbering under
the blossoming citron-bush. And the young men think
of Palosara, who, by his unassisted arm, won a royal
bride and the kingdom of Ngastina.

# ON THE BEACH

THE million-footed crowd of travelling humanity has trodden Tandjong Priok out of all beauty and pleasantness. It is nothing now but a heap of dust rendered compact by a coating of basalt and bricks, and bearing on its flat surface some half-dozen square squat sheds, the whitewashed walls of which glare intolerably in the sunlight that beats upon the barren place all day long. But a little further down the shore, eastwards from the harbour, the natural beauty of the country re-asserts itself. There are wide, shallow bays, where the water sleeps in the shadow of overhanging trees; sandy points, one projecting beyond the other across shimmering intervals of sea; and alternating with open spaces, where a few bamboo-huts are clustered together amidst a plantation of young banana trees, great tracts of woodland, that come down to the very margin of the water. In one place where the narrow beach broadens out a little, some half dozen shanties, one of which might, by courtesy, be styled a bathing-lodge, have found standing-room between the wood and the water. Some homesick exile from France has christened the handful of bamboo-posts and atap-leaves: Petite Trouville. In the dry season, when Batavia is parched with heat and choked with dust, people come hither for a plunge into the clear cool waves, and for some hours of blissful idleness in the shadow of the broad-branched nyamploeng trees, which mirror their dark leafage and clusters of white wax-like blossoms in the tide.

The day, some friends took me to see the place, was one of the last in April, when the rains were not yet quite over. We had left Batavia at half-past five, when the Koningsplein was still white with rolling mists and the stars had but just begun to fade in the greyish sky. The train had borne us along some distance on our way to Tandjong Priok, ere the sun rose. Rather, ere it appeared. There had been no heralding change of colour in the eastern sky; only the uncertain light that lay over the landscape had gradually strengthened; and all at once, at some height above the horizon a triangular splendour burst forth, a great heart of flame which was the sun. The pools and tracts of marshy ground flooded by the recent rains were ridged with long straight parallel lines of red. The dark tufts of palm-trees here and there shone like burnished bronze. And where they grew denser, in groups and little groves, the blue mist hanging between the stems was pierced by lances of reddish light.

At Tandjong Priok station, we alighted amidst a crowd of natives, dock-labourers and coal-heavers, on their way to the ships. They took the road in true native style, one marching behind the other, laughing and talking as they went. And we followed them, in our jolting sadoos, along a sunny avenue, planted with slim young trees, as far as to the bend of the road; then we left it and entered the wood on the right, which we had for some time been skirting.

A rough track led through it. Our sadoos jolted worse than ever in the ruts left by the broad-wheeled carts of the peasantry. We alighted and made our way as best we could through the grass-grown clearings of the jungle. The sun was but just beginning to warm the air. White shreds of mist still hung among the tree-stems, and swathed the brushwood. The grass underfoot was white with dew, glistening with myriads of brilliant little points, where the yellow sunlight touched it. The broadly curved banana leaves, and the feathery tufts of the palm trees overhead began to grow transparent, standing out in light green against the shining white-ness of the sky. There was an inexpressible vitality and exhilaration in all things, in the fine pure air, cool as well-water, in the sparkle of the dew-lit grass, in the bushes with large round drops trembling on every leaf, in the pungent scent of the lantana, that on every side displayed its clusters of pink, mauve and orange red blossoms. It was good to feel wet-through on the tramp through the drenched tangle, to feel the blood tingling in the finger tips, the lungs full of quickening air, and the sunshine right in your eyes. It was good to be alive.

After a while, we came to a little campong, some five or six bamboo huts, grouped together in an open space of the wood. Some naked children were playing around a fire of sticks and dry leaves. Under a shed, a woman stood pounding rice in a hollowed-out wooden block, whilst another, carrying a child in her slendang, talked to her. There were no men about, save one old fellow, white-haired and decrepid, who sat in his door-way, mending nets in that sunny forest-clearing, that was the one thing suggestive of the neighbouring sea.

Past the village there are several tanks of brackish

water, where fish is bred for Chinese consumption. Tangles of green weed floated on the surface, which, in places, seemed to be filmed over with oily colours. A man walked along the shore, dredging. Beyond, the wood recommenced. But it was less dense there; great patches of sunlight lay on the ground, and the sky showed everywhere through the stems. As we issued out of the dappled shade, we beheld the sea.

Calm and clear, it lay under the calm clear sky, a silvery splendour suffused in places with the faintest blue. Not a ripple disturbed the lustrous smoothness. Only, out in the open, the water heaved with a scarcely perceptible swell, its rise and subsidence revealed by a rhythmic pulsation of colour—streaks of pale turquoise breaking out upon the pearly monochrome, kindling into azure and gradually fainting and fading again. To the westward the mole of Tandjong Priok and the two bar-iron light-towers, standing seemingly close together, had dwindled to a narrow dark line with, at its extreme point, two little black filigree figures delicately defined against the shimmering white of sea and sky. Near the shore, a fishing-prao, its slight hull almost disappearing under the immense white winglike sail, lay still above its motionless reflection. In the eastern distance, a group of island, ethereal as cloudlets, hung where the sheen of the sea and the shimmer of the sky flowed together into one tremulous splendour, dazzling and colourless. The beach, with a nipah-thatched hut on the right and a group of spreading njamploeng trees on the left, framed the radiant vista with sober browns and greens.

The morning was still, without a breath of air; and all around the foliage hung motionless. Yet, as we walked over the fine grey sand, which already felt hot under foot, there came drifting down to us now and again, whiffs of a sweet subtle fragrance, as of March violets; and transparent blossoms, fluttering down, whitened the shell-strown beach. Then jamploengs were in flower.

Looking at that dark-leaved grove on the margin of the water, I thought I had seldom seen nobler trees. Not very tall; but round and broad, great hemispheres of foliage squarely supported on column-like trunks. In their general air and bearing, in the character of the oblong leaves and their elegant poise upon the branch, they somewhat resemble the walnuts of northern countries. The colour is even richer, a vigorous bluish green, swarthy at a distance; and when seen near at hand, as full of tender beryl-tints as a field of young oats, with watery gleams and glories playing through the depths of the foliage. For a crowning grace, the njamploeng has its blossoms, fragrant, white, and of a wax-like transparency—cups of milky light. Standing under an ancient tree, that overhung the water with trailing branches and a tangle of wave-washed roots, I could see the luminous clusters shining in that dome of dusky leafage, like stars in an evening sky. And the water in the shadow gleamed with pale reflections.

The sea, that morning, passed through a succession of chromatic changes. The silvery smoothness of an hour ago had been broken by a ripple, that came and went in dashes of ruffled ultra-marine. Then, here and there, purplish patches appeared, which presently began to spread until they touched, and flowed together, and the sea, all along the shore, seemed turned to muddy wine, whilst, out in the open, it sparkled in a rich blue-green, rippling and flickering. At noon, the purplish brown had disappeared, and the emerald-like tints had faded and changed to an uncertain olive-green. The sky as yet retained its morning aspect, cloudless and shimmering with a white brilliancy as if all the stars of the Milky Way had been dissolved in it. Under that enduring paleness, the fitful colouring and flushing of the sea seemed all the stranger.

As the day advanced, the heat had steadily increased, and at last it was intolerable. About ten, when we swam out into the sea, the water, even where it grew deeper, felt tepid; a little after noon it was warm. The windless air quivered. And the sand was so hot as to scorch our bare feet when we attempted to step out of the circular shadow of the njamploengs, where a little coolness as yet remained.

A dead quiet lay on sea and land. There was neither wind nor wave, not the thinnest shadow of a sailing cloud, to temper for an instant the unbearable glare. The foliage overhead was the one spot of colour in a white-hot universe. There must be cicadas among the leaves: I had heard them trilling, earlier in the day; but the heat had reduced them to silence. Even the black ants, crawling among the roots, and in the fissures of the rough rind of the trees seemed to move but listlessly. From where I sat, I could see, framed by the circular sweep of the hanging foliage, a stretch of beach, with some huts amidst a banana-plantation, and further down a native boat lying keel upwards upon the sand. A lean dog crouched in the shadow, panting with tongue hanging out. No other living creature was to be seen.

The afternoon was far gone before there came a change, imperceptible at first, a gradual sobering of colour, and a growing definiteness in the contours of trees and bushes. Then the air began to cool down.

The horizon grew distinct; a curve of rich green against sunlit blue; a short ripple roughened the water; and suddenly, the breeze sprang up, driving before it a wave that hurried and rose, and broke foaming upon the beach. The tide was coming in.

It was as if the inspiriting hour that changed the face of land and sea, made itself felt also in the little brown huts under the trees, stirring up the folk into briskness and activity. Merry voices and the cries of children mingled with the sound of hammer-strokes, reverberating along the wooded beach. Among the trees I could discern the figure of a man bending over his boat, tool in hand; and a woman coming out of her door with a bundle of clothes under one arm. Where the lengthening shadow of the njamploeng trees fell on the sunny water, two young girls were bathing; somewhat further down, a swarm of naked urchins waded through the shallows, in search of mother-of-pearl. The yellow sunlight shone on their little brown bodies and made the ripples sparkle around them as they splashed hither and thither, feeling about with their feet for the flat sharp shards which the tide leaves buried in the sands. Standing still for an instant, when they had found one, they balanced on one foot, whilst with the clenched toes of the other they picked up the shiny piece with a supple, monkey-like movement. Presently, along came an old man in a straw topee broad-rimmed hat and a faded reddish sarong, who entered the sea and waded towards the spot, where, that morning—when it was as yet dry land— he had erected his "tero," the piable bamboo palisade, which, arranged in the shape of a V, with the opening towards the shore, serves as a trap for fish. The hurdle was all but overflowed now, only the points of the

bamboo stakes emerging above the rising tide, like the
rigging of some wrecked and sunken ship. The old
man gave it a shake, to assure himself of having driven
it deep enough down into the sand to withstand the
impact of the waves; and satisfied upon this point,
limped away again, with the air of a man who had
finished his day's work. He might lie down on his
baleh-baleh now, and peacefully smoke his cigarette.
Whilst he was taking his ease, the sea would provide
for his daily fish. In a few minutes the tide would
have submerged his „tero," and the heedless fish would
swim across it; and as the water ebbed away again,
they would be driven against the converging sides of
the lattice-work, and presently be left gasping upon
the bars. Then the women of the village would come
with their baskets, and gather the living harvest, as
they might a windfall of ripe fruit; and his grandson,
out at sea now, with the other young men, would hang
two full baskets to his bending yoke, and with the
fire-car go to Batavia, there to sell the fish for much
money, a handful of copper doits. Even if he had
caught "kabak" which the orang blandah like, and
"gabus," of which the rich Chinese are fond, the boy
might bring him home some silver coins. And his
grand-daughter would salt and dry in the sun the
smaller fry, and make "ikan kring" for him and all
the household.

Happy the man who has dutiful children! In his
old age, when he is able no longer to earn his sustenance, he will not want; he need not beg nor
borrow from the kampong folk; and he will not be
tempted to invoke Kjaï Belorong, the wicked goddess
of wealth, who, in exchange for riches, demands men's
souls. Do not all in this kampong know of Pah-Sidin,

and what became of him after he had prayed to the evil sprite? Here is the tale, as the old fisherman gave it me.

He was a poor man, Pah-Sidin, unlucky in whatever he undertook and so utterly ignorant as not to know one single "ilmu." * So that, though his wife worked from morning till night, weaving and batikking sarongs, and tending the garden and the field, and selling fruit and flowers, things went from bad to worse with him. And at last there was not a grain of rice left in the house, and the green crop in the field was the property of the usurer. His wife, weeping, said: "O Pah-Sidin! how now shall we feed and clothe our little ones, Sidin, and all the others?" But he, vexed with her importunities, and weary of fasting and going about in faded clothes without a penny to buy sirih or pay his place at a cock-fight, said: "Be silent! for I know where to find great wealth." Then he went away, and walked along the shore for many days, until he came to a place where there were great rocks and caves in which the water made a sound as of thunder. Here lives the dread goddess, Njai Loro Kidul, the Virgin Queen of the Southern Seas, whom the gatherers of edible birds' nest invoke, honouring her with sacrifices before they set out on their perilous quest. And here too, lives her servant, wicked Kjaï Belorong, the money-goddess.

Pah-Sidin standing in the entrance of a black and thunderous cave, strewed kanangan flowers and melatih, and yellow champaka, and burnt costly frankincense, and as the cloud of fragrant smoke ascended, he fell on his face and cried: "Kjaï Belorong! I invoke thee! I am poor and utterly wretched! Do thou give me money,

* Charm to conjure good fortune.

and I will give thee my soul, O Kjaï Belorong!" Then a voice, which caused the blood to run cold in his veins, answered: "I hear thee, Pah-Sidin." He arose, trembling, and as he turned his head, saw that the cave was a house, large and splendid and full of golden treasure. But as he looked closer, behold! It was built of human bodies; floor, walls and roof all made of living men, who wept and groaned, crying: "Alas, alas! who can endure these unendurable pains!" And the horrible voice, speaking for the second time, asked: "Pah-Sidin, hast thou courage?"

Pah-Sidin, at first, seemed as though he would have fainted with horror. But soon, reflecting how he was young and strong, and the hour of his death far off as yet, and hoping also, that in the end he might be able to deceive Kjaï Belorong and save his soul, whilst in the meanwhile he would enjoy great honour and riches, he answered; "Kjaï Belorong, I have courage!" And the voice spoke for the third time: "It is well! Go back to thine own house now; for soon I will come to thee."

So Pah-Sidin returned to his house, and waited for Kjaï Belorong, saying nothing of the matter to his wife. And in the night she came, and sat upon the baleh-baleh, and said: "Embrace me Pah-Sidin, for now I am thy love." Pah-Sidin would willingly have kissed her, for she seemed as fair as the bride of the love-god. But looking down, he saw that, instead of legs and feet, she had a long scaly tail; then he was afraid, and would have fled. But Kjaï Belorong, seizing him in her arms, said: "If thou but triest to escape, I will kill thee," and she pressed him to her bosom so violently that the breath forsook his body, and he lay as one dead. Then she loosened her grasp and disappeared, rattling her tail. But when Pah-Sidin returned to consciousness, he saw in the faint light of the dawn, the baleh-baleh all strewn with yellow scales, and each scale was a piece of the finest gold.

Pah-Sidin now was as the richest Rajah: he had a splendid house with granaries and stables, fine horses, great plantations of palms and jambus and all other kinds of fruit, and rich *sawahs* that stretched as far as a man on horseback could see. He abandoned his wife, who was no longer young and was worn out with care and labour; and married the daughter of a wealthy Rajah, and three other maidens as fair as bidadaris. And whenever he wished for more money, Kjaï Belorong came to him in the night and embraced him, and gave him more than he had asked for. Thus the years went by in great glory and happiness, until the hair of his head began to grow white, and his eyes lost their brilliancy, and his black and shining teeth fell out. Then, one night, Kjaï Belorong came to his couch, unsummoned, looked at him and said: "Pah-Sidin! the hour is come. Follow me and I will make thee the threshold of my palace." But Pah-Sidin made answer and said: "Alas! Kjaï Belorong! look at me, how lean I am! My ribs almost pierce through the skin of my side. Assuredly, thou wilt hurt thy tail in passing over me, if thou makest me the threshold of thy house. Rather take with thee my plough-boy, who is young, and plump, and smooth!"

Then Kjaï Belorong took the plough-boy. And Pah-Sidin married a new wife, and lived merrier than before. Thus ten years went by in great glory and happiness. But on the last night of the tenth year, Kjaï Belorong again came to his couch, unsummoned, and looked at him and said: "Pah-Sidin! the hour is come. Follow

me, and I will make thee the pillar of my palace."
But Pah-Sidin made answer and said: "Alas! Kjaï
Belorong! look at me, how weak I am! My shoulders
are so bent, I can scarcely keep the badju-jacket from
gliding down. Assuredly, thy roof will fall in and crush
thee, if thou makest me the pillar of thy house. Rather
take with thee my youngest brother, who is strong
and tall, and broad of shoulders!"

Then Kjaï Belorong took the brother. But Pah-Sidin
married yet another new wife, and lived even merrier
than hitherto. Thus ten more years went by in great
glory and happiness. But on the last night of the tenth
year, Kjaï Belorong for the third time came to his
couch, unsummoned, looked at him and spoke: "Pah-
Sidin! the hour is come. Follow me, and I will make
thee the hearth-stone of my palace!" And Pah-Sidin
made answer and said: "Alas! Kjaï Belorong! look at
me, how cold I am and covered all over with a clammy
sweat! Assuredly thy fire will smoulder and go out
if thou makest me the hearthstone of thy house. Rather
take with thee my eldest son, Sidin, who is healthy,
and warm, and dry!" But the wicked Kjaï Belorong,
in a voice which made Pah-Sidin's heart stand still,
screamed: "I will take none but thee, old man! and
since thou art so cold and wet, I will bid my imperish-
able fire warm and dry thee!" And with these words
the demon seized Pah-Sidin by the throat, and carried
him off to her horrible abode, there to be the stone
upon which her hearth-fire burns everlastingly."

At the conclusion of this long tale, the old fisherman
drew a sigh of relief. "Such is the fate of those who
let themselves be conquered by greed and the wiles of
wicked Kjaï Belorong. But I, njonja, need have no fear.
For my children are dutiful, and provide for all my

wants. Nor need any one else in this dessa fear. For we are all pious men, who pray to the Prophet and the Toewan Allah. Thus we are safe."

Indeed, to judge from the appearance of these good-natured, frugal and careless people, I should have fancied that the money-goddess could not make many victims among them.

But their safety is threatened by yet another enemy, — a much more energetic one than Kjaï Belorong to all appearance: to wit "My Lord the Crocodile." The coast swarms with these brutes; and according to official reports, quite a number of people are annually devoured by them.

They infest especially the marshy country around the mouth of the Kali Batawi, where they may sometimes be seen, lying half in the water and half upon a mud-bank, their wicked little eyes blinking in the sunlight, their formidable jaws agape and showing the bright yellow of the gullet. There they wait for the carcases of drowned animals and the offal of all kinds floating down the river. Imprudent bathers are often attacked by them, and they even swim up the water-courses, and venture for considerable distances inland.

The Government, some years ago, put a premium on the capture of crocodiles, a relatively high sum being offered for a carcase. But the measure had to be withdrawn after a while, and this, though to all appearance it worked excellently well. Numbers of crocodiles were caught and killed; not a day went by but natives presented themselves at the police stations, exhibiting a limp carcase slung on to a bamboo frame, which a score of coolies "pikoled" * along. Harassed officials began to believe in a universe peopled exclusively by

* To pikol = to carry a load slung on a pole.

Malays and dead or dying crocodiles; and philanthropists
rejoiced over an imminent extermination of caymans
and the consequent safety for bathers. But there were
those who understood the nature of both natives and
crocodiles, and who considered their ways; and they
smiled a smile of wisdom and ineffable pity, as they
looked upon the dead saurians, and saw that they were
young. The philanthropists contended that a little crocodile was a crocodile nevertheless, and would in its own
bad time, be a big crocodile and one which feasted on
the flesh of men and women and innocent children;
but those wise men only smiled the more. And presently
one of them took a philanthropist by the hand, and led
him by quiet waters, and showed him how men and
women sought for the eggs of the crocodile, and gathered them in their bosom, and watched the young come
out, and reared them even with a father's care and
loving-kindness, to the end that they might wax fat
and kick, and be bound with iron chains, and delivered
over to the schout.*

The crocodiles now are left to multiply and replenish
the shores of Java; and nobody molests them, except
now and then some adventurous sportsman, upon whom
tigers have palled, and who cares but little for "ban-
tengs,"† and holds the rhinoceros of no account. And
generally too, though he lie in wait for a crocodile, he
catches only a fever—of a particularly malignant kind,
it is true.

The Malays, as a rule, do not readily kill crocodiles.
They believe that the spirits of the dead are re-incarnated
in these animals; so that, what seems a repulsive and
dangerous beast, may, in reality, be an honoured father,
or a long lamented bride. And they piously prefer the

---

* A police official.    † The wild buffalo.

risk of being devoured to the certainty of becoming
murderers  Far from injuring, they honour the "cayman"
by sacrifices of rice, meat and fruit, which they send
down the river in little baskets of palm-leaves with a
light twinkling a-top; a gift offered whenever a child
is born, to propitiate the metamorphosed ancestors in
river and sea, and implore their protection for this,
their newly born descendant.  Human feelings and
susceptibilities are attributed to them, which the Malay
carefully abstains from wounding. He never speaks but
of "My Lord the Crocodile." And a wayang-play, such
as, for instance, Krokosono, the hero of which defeats
and kills the King of the Crocodiles, no dalang would
dream of representing in a place where caymans could
hear or see it.  There is one act however, by which a
crocodile forfeits all claim to respect : and that is killing
a human being. From his supposed human nature it
evidently follows, that this is an act of malice prepense,
a crime knowingly committed; and as such, should be
punished as it would be were the perpetrator a man
or a woman—that is, with death. It would seem too,
as if the guilty creature were conscious of his crime,
and sometimes, out of sheer remorse, gave himself up
to justice. At least, a story to this effect is told of a
certain crocodile, which had devoured a little girl, and
this, though the child's parents had duly offered rice
and meat and fruit at the stated times; of which gifts
this crocodile had undoubtedly had his share. The parents,
weeping, sought a hermit who lived not far from the
"dessa" or village, a wise man who understood the
language of animals; and implored him to restore at
least the remains of their daughter's little body to them,
and to visit with condign punishment her brutal murderer.
The hermit, moved with pity and indignation, forthwith

left his cave, and repaired to the sea-shore. There, standing with his feet in the waves, he pronounced the potent spell which all crocodiles must obey. They came hurrying from far and near: the shore bristled with their scaly backs ranged in serried rank and file. When all were present, the hermit addressed them in their own tongue, declaring that one of them had committed the unpardonable crime of murder, murder upon an innocent child, whose parents had offered sacrifices for her at her birth: rice and fruit and meat, of which they all had partaken in token of amity and good will. So abominable a breach of good faith should not be suffered to remain unpunished. Wherefore, let him who had perpetrated it, stand forth! But all the others, let them withdraw into the sea! The crocodiles heard. The solid land seemed to heave and break up, as the congregated thousands dispersed. But one crocodile remained behind on the beach. It crawled nearer and lay down at the feet of the hermit. And the father of the little girl, approaching, drew his "kris," and thrust it into the creature's eyes, killing it. The holy man then took out of the monster's jaws the necklace of blue beads, which the little girl had worn, and handed it to the father, promising him that, within the year, his wife would bear him another daughter, even fairer than the lost one. But the carcase of the crocodile was devoured by the dogs.

Something in the landscape near Petite Trouville brought back to my memory this tale, heard from a village priest some time ago. It was a fit scene for such events. That brown hut among the bananas might have been the abode of the hapless little maid. The dense wood behind, might well shelter an anchorite, some old man, wise and humble, content to live on

wild fruit and learn from the birds among the branches
and the fish in the sea; assuredly he would stand
upon the little spit of land that has the njamploeng
on it, and the crocodiles, obedient to his command,
would raise their formidable heads from the water, and
with their serried ranks cover the shelving beach.......
Very peaceful it lay now in the light of the setting
sun.  The sea shone golden.  And already, among the
blossom-laden branches of the njamploeng, there began
to rustle the sea-breeze, precursor of deepbreathed Night.

OF BUITENZORG

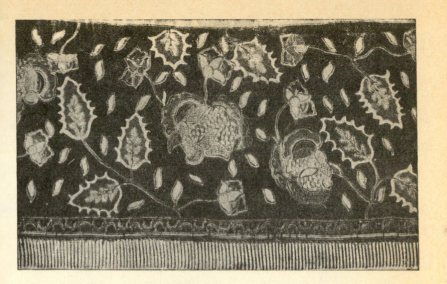

The Javanese Sans-Souci * lies cradled in a fold of
the undulating country at the base of the Salak, whose
blue top, twin to that of the Gedeh, is seen in fine
weather, from the Koningsplein, rising aerially, fresh
and pure above the dusty glare of Batavia. The village
is pretty,—all brown atap houses and gardens full of
roses, with the wooded hill-side for a background.
One may wander for hours in the splendid Botanical
Garden, reputed to be the finest in the world, and a
goal of pilgrimage for scientists from every part of the
globe. Whoever visits the place in September may
combine these tranquil pleasures with the gaiety of
the annual races, and the great ball at the Buitenzorg
Club, where "all Java" dances. I went in the last
week of the month, glad to escape from the town,
which, at this time of the year, is unbearable, scorched
with the heat of the east monsoon and stifled under

* Buitenzorg, literally translated, means "away from sorrow or care."

a layer of dust, which makes the grass of the gardens crumble away, and turns the "assam" trees along the river and in the squares into grey spectres. The country through which the first part of my road lay, seemed however scarcely desolate. Nothing but flat monotonous fields, some altogether bare and grey, others still covered with yellowish stubble, through which the cracks and fissures of the parched soil showed. Here and there a patch of green, where some huddled brown roofs and a group of thin palm-trees denoted a native hamlet, forlorn in the wide arid plain. Then again, bare brown fields, where no living creature was to be seen, except now and then a herd of dun buffaloes wallowing in the ooze of some dried-up pool.

By and bye however, the character of the landscape began to change. The rich blue-green of the young rice-crops, seen first in isolated squares and patches, spread all over the gradually-ascending fields. Along the course of a rapid rivulet, a bamboo grove sprang up, lithe stems bending a little under their cascades of waving dull-green foliage. Then the rice-clad undulations of the ground began to rise into little hills, green to the very top, and down the sides of which the water, that fed the terraced fields trickled in many a twisting silvery thread; and suddenly on the left, rose the great triangular mass of the Salak, dull-blue in the sober evening-light. It was almost dark when the train stopped at the Buitenzorg station. It stands at some distance from the village; and as I drove thither, sights and sounds reached me that denoted the hilly country. The wheels of the cab creaked over whitish pebbles, clean as gravel from the rocky river-bed. The gardens on each side the road were full of flowers, that gleamed palely through the semi-darkness.

Buffaloes at grass.

Avenue leading to the Botanical Garden.

The voices of passers-by, the laughter of children at play, the tones of a flute somewhere in the distance, sounded clear and far through the thinner air. As I entered the village, I noticed that the houses were built of bamboo instead of the brick, which is the usual material in the clayey lowlands.

It is said that these bamboo houses, covered with atap, withstand the shock of earthquakes, frequent in this country, much better than brick buildings with tiled roofs. However that may be, their rural aspect harmonizes with the landscape: and they are delightful to inhabit, cool under the noonday heat, and proof against the torrential rains, which, at Buitenzorg, fall every day between two and four in the afternoon. I lived for some time in a little pavilion,—wooden floor, pagar walls and a roof of atap; a pleasanter abode I never knew. It was almost like living in a hermit's cell out in the woods. I was never sure whether the soft creaking noises heard all night through, came from the bamboo grove in the garden, or from the bamboo in my wall. The crickets seemed to sing in my very ears; and a faint, sweet smell pervaded the little room, such as breathes from the leafage, dead and living, of a forest. Like a cenobite's cell too, my pavilion was not meant for a storehouse of worldly treasures. Even if moths and rust did not corrupt, thieves would have quite exceptional facilities for breaking through and stealing them. "Breaking through" is too energetic and vigorous a term; with an ordinary penknife, one might cut away enough of the walls to admit a battalion of burglars. Reading one day a French translation of Don Quixote, I rested the ponderous folio, which tired my arms, against the wall. It instantly gave way, sinking in, as if it had been a canvas awning. I do not doubt that, with my embroidery scissors, I might have cut out an elegant open-work pattern in it.

The morning after my arrival I was up betimes and on my way to the Botanical Garden. It was early as yet, a little after sunrise, and the air felt as cool and as pure as well-water. A frost-like dew had whitened the grass; shreds of mist hung between the trees, trailed along the hillside, and floated like low white clouds in the depths of the ravine, where the river foamed past over the boulders of its rocky bed. And in the branches, the birds were twittering and singing their little hearts out. I met some natives on the way to their morning-bath hugging themselves in the folds of the "baju," the women among them having the "slendang" drawn over their heads. They walked at a brisk pace, very different from the listless movements of pedestrians in the sultry streets of Batavia. The type was of another kind, a slightly oval face, with a thin nose somewhat aquiline in design, and very brilliant eyes; the complexion of a clear yellowish brown, with a touch of red in the lips. They had an elastic gait, and the free carriage of the head peculiar to hillfolk. Some of the young girls were absolutely pretty.

I asked my way of an old woman who sat by the roadside, complacently smoking a cigarette, and soon found myself within the gates of the Botanical Garden, and in the celebrated waringin avenue, one of the glories of the place. The first impression, I confess, is somewhat disappointing. The avenue is not very long, so that it lacks the depths of green darkness, the prospect along apparently converging parallels of pillar-like trunks, and the bluish shimmer of light afar off, which are the characteristic charms of woodland glades. It seems more like a square, planted with trees on two sides of the quadrangle only, a comparatively narrow space of shadow, abutting on the broad fields of sunlight beyond. After a while however, one notices the smallness of the figures moving past the trees, men, horses, and bullock-carts. By comparison, one begins to realize the gigantic proportions of it all,—the length and breadth and height of the leafy vault overhead, and the hugeness of those stupendous growths that support it, each of them a grove in itself, congregated hundreds of trees, group by group of stately stems crowding round the colossal parent bole. Then, bye and bye, the sense of grandeur

is succeeded by a curious impression of lifelessness. In their vast size, their stark immobility, and their rigid attitudes, these grey masses resemble granite peaks and cliffs rather than trees. The aged trunks, broadbased, are riven and fissured like weather-beaten rocks, showing gnarled protuberances and black clefts from which ferns and mosses droop. Some, rotten to the core— nothing left of the trunk but a fragment of grey gnarled rind, with the fungus-overgrown mould, lying heaped up against the base—resemble boulders, covered with earth and detritus. One or two, quite decayed, hang in mid-air, dependent from a dome of interlacing branches, stems and air-roots, like some gigantic stalactite from the roof of a pillared cavern. And aloft, the dense masses of foliage, grey against the sunlit brilliancy of the sky, seem like the broken and crumbling vault of this immense grotto. This strange resemblance of living vegetable matter to inert stone ceases only when, issuing from among the stems, one looks at the waringins from a distance, and sees the grey multitude of boles, trunks and stems disappearing under spreading masses of foliage, resplendent in the sun.

The garden is worthy of this magnificent entrance.

A Hill-man.

Enthusiastic "savants" have sung its praises in all the languages of civilization, and by common consent, have declared it to be the finest botanical garden in the world, assigning the second place to famous Kew, and mentioning the gardens of Berlin, Paris, and Vienna as third, fourth,

In the depth of the ravine.

The Brantas River.  Malang.

and fifth in order of merit. Originally, it was no more than the park belonging to the country-house, which Governor-General Van Imhoff built here in 1754: a house since destroyed by an earth-quake, and on the site of which the present lodge was erected.

In this park, Professor Bernwardt, some eighty years ago, arranged a small botanical garden, a "hortus" as

Watch-men.

the innocent pedantry of the period called it. The idea was to gather in this fertile spot specimens of all the plants and trees growing in Java, so as to afford men of science an opportunity for studying the flora of the island. By and bye however, especially under the direction of Teysmann, many plants from other countries were introduced, with a view of acclimatizing them in

Java, often with signal success. And recently, a museum and a library have been established, as well as several laboratories for chemical, botanical and pharmaceutical research. For the cultivation of such plants as require a cool climate, gardens have been laid out on the terraced hill-side, in ascending tiers that climb up to

Prinsenlaan-corner, Batavia.

the heights of Tji-Bodas, where in the early morning, the temperature is 10° Celsius. These ameliorations for the greater part are due to the untiring energy of the eminent scientist now directing the garden.

But that morning, as I wandered through the tall avenues of the Buitenzorg Park, the thought of its im-

The beautiful tall reeds of the sugar cane, their pennon-like leaves gleaming in the sunshine.

Avenue of old waringin trees. Botanical Garden, Buitenzorg.

portance as a scientific institution disappeared before the perception of its exquisite loveliness. Not a beauty of line and colour merely: it has these—the park is admirably arranged, in broad effects of light and shadow, dark hued groves and avenues contrasting with sunny expanses of lawn and copse and mirroring lake; but there is something over and above all this, an element of beauty as subtle and elusive as the transient sparkle of a sun-beam, or the fitful comings and goings of the summer wind. Perhaps it was the extraordinary brilliancy of the colours, and the shimmer in the rain-saturated atmosphere; or perhaps it was the profound quietude all around, a stillness so perfect that it seemed it must endure for ever. I do not know what may have been the elements that made up the nameless charm. But I yielded myself up to it; and it seemed to me, as if I were walking in a dream, amidst objects at once unreal and singularly distinct. For a long time I sat by the shore of a little lake, that had an islet in the midst of it, all overgrown with brushwood, and great tangles of liana, that opened hundreds of pale violet flowers to the sunlight; in the centre there rose a group of young palms of the sort that has a bright red stem; and all these colours, the many-tinted green and the lilac and the scarlet were mirrored so vividly in the clear water as to almost make the reflection seem brighter than the reality.... By and by, following a path that wandered out of sunshine into chequered shadow, and out of shadow into sunlight again, I came to a vast sweep of meadowy ground, where herds of reddish deer were feeding as peacefully as in a forest clearing. Presently I found myself in a great dim avenue of kenari-trees, through whose sombre branches the sky showed but faintly;

and anon in a bamboo grove, where there was a continual rustling and waving of leaves though not the

A cactus in flower.

slightest breath of wind could be felt to stir the air.
Here and there through gaps in the trees came a
sudden glimpse of the distant valley, with the river

Gum tree, Botanical Garden, Buitenzorg.

Palm trees in the Botanical Garden.

shining between the light-green rice fields, and beyond
the encircling hills. Everywhere too, the presence of
living water made itself felt, in the cool damp air, and
in the delicious smell of moist earth, wet stones and
water-plants. And I would suddenly catch the silvery
gleams, between the bushes, of a brooklet hurrying
past over its pebbly bed, and foaming in small cascades
that be-sprinkled the ferns and tall nodding grasses
upon the bank with scintillating spray. Here and
there I heard the murmur and tinkle of a fountain;
and I passed by quiet ponds and lakelets, dark green
in the shadow of overhanging trees. One of these
sheets of water—or rather the streamlet into which it
narrows at one end—is completely overgrown with
white lotus flowers; and a sight more exquisitely beautiful cannot be imagined. It burst upon me suddenly,
as I came out of a long, dark avenue; and at first, I
could not make out what that white splendour was.
It seemed to float like a luminous summer-cloud, like a
snowy drift of morning mist. A breath of wind arose,
and the even splendour trembled and seemed to break
up into hundreds of white flames and sparks, that for
an instant all blew one way, and then shot up again,
and stood steadily shining. As I came nearer, I discerned
the great, round white flowers, radiant in the sunshine.
The circular, purplish brown leaves spread all over the
surface of the water, covering it from bank to bank.
And out of these heaps of bronze shields, there rose
the straight tall stems, like lances, with the white flame
of the flower breaking out at the top—sparks, of
St. Elmo's fire, such as, on that memorable night, tipped
the spears of the Roman cohorts, on their march to
battle and victory.

This field of radiant lotus blossoms, and the sombre

and solemn waringin avenue, contrasting glories, seem
to me to be the crowning beauties of the Buitenzorg

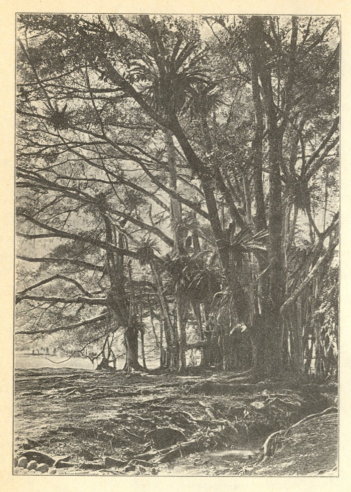

A waringin-tree.

garden. The name of Buitenzorg, by the bye, is an
innovation. Natives still call the town by its ancient
name of Bogor, which it bore in the glorious age when

A path leading from sunshine into dappled shade and from shade into sunshine again.

A bamboo-grove where was an incessant rustling and waving of foliage though no wind.

it was the capital of the Hindoo realm of Padjadjaran A Muslim conqueror, Hassan Udin, son of the Sheik Mulana, destroyed it; and a new town was reared on the ruins, but legends of its bygone glory still haunt the imagination of the country folk. In the tales which they repeat to one another of an evening, the splendour of the ancient empire and the wisdom and unconquerable valour of its founder are still remembered. Tjioeng

Carriers walking by the side of their lumbering, bullock-drawn pedati, which creaks along the sun-scorched roads.

Wonara was his name; and his son and successor, the victorious Praboe Wangi, was even greater than he. In the craggy hill-tops of the Gedeh-range, popular tradition sees the ruins of the splendid palace he built himself on the heights; the hall where the throne of gold and ivory stood; the temple, where he worshipped the gods; the domes of his harem; and the battlemented towers which his unconquerable warriors kept against the world, a thousand years ago. The southern wall of the Gedeh-crater surrounds, as an impregnable bulwark, the palace and temple courts.

The Hindoo period however, has left in this neighbourhood records more authentic than Praboe Wangi's fancy-built palace on the heights. Near a native kampong, which derives its name from this proximity, the so-called Batu Tulis is found, a field covered with a quantity of stone slabs, some lying prone, others still upright, adorned with figures in bas-relief and covered with inscriptions. The legend on the largest of these memorial tablets, traced in ancient Javanese characters, has been deciphered; it celebrates the virtues and victories of a Hindoo king. And the worn-away superscriptions and rude effigies discernible on the other stones probably commemorate contemporary princes and warriors. The Bogor country-folk greatly venerate these relics of a glorious past.

Carriers walking by the side of their lumbering bullock-drawn "pedati," which creaks so leisurely along the sun-scorched roads; labourers on their way to the rice-fields, the light wooden ploughshare across their shoulders, driving the patient yoke of oxen before them; women from the hill-villages around, who come to the Bogor market in holiday attire, a chaplet of jessamine blossoms twisted into their "kondeh"—all turn aside from the road, to murmur a short prayer, and offer a handful of flowers, of frankincense and yellow boreh unguent, or even Chinese joss-sticks and small paper lanterns on the consecrated spot. Whether this be an act of homage to those ancient kings and heroes, whose rude effigies adorn the stones, and whose spirits are believed still to haunt the spot; or simply a fetishistic adoration of these blocks of granite and the curious signs engraved thereon, it is difficult to decide; the

Palm trees and Arancaria.

A tall gloomy avenue of kenari trees, the sky but faintly showing through their sombre branches.

worshippers themselves hardly seem to know. When
asked, they reply that they do as their fathers did before
them, and so therefore must be right; unless indeed,
they merely smile, and offer the somewhat irrelevant
remark that they are true Moslemin. This indeed,
every native of Java (save such few as have been

Submerged rice-field.

converted to the Christian religion) professes himself to
be. And, in a measure, the Javanese are Mohammedans;
they recite the Mohammedan prayers and Confession of
Faith, go to the Messigit—which is Javanese for mosqué—
when it suits them, keep the Ramadan very strictly;
also, if they can afford it, they perform that most sacred
duty of the Mohammedan, the Mecca pilgrimage, and

returning thence, live for ever on the purses of their
admiring co-religionists. But for the rest, one may apply
to them Napoleon's dictum concerning the Russians—
mutatis mutandis —: Scratch the Muslim and you will
find the Hindoo; scratch the Hindoo, and you will find
the fetish-adoring Pagan. In the same way too, as they
confuse religious beliefs, they distort historical facts and
traditions so as to make them tally with the prevalent
opinions of the day. This Batu Tulis, for instance:
though they venerate it as a record of the Hindoo
empire, they yet, at the same time, honour it as a
monument of the Mohammedan conquest. According
to them, these roughly-fashioned stones, of which, they
say, there are over eight hundred dispersed throughout
the neighbourhood, are the transformed shapes of
Siliwangi, last King of Padjadjaran, and his followers,
who, in this spot, their last refuge on flight from the
victorious Muslim hosts, were turned into stones by Tuan
Allah, as a punishment for their persistent refusal to
embrace El-Islam; and the superscription celebrating the
Hindoo-prince, they make out to be the record of this
miracle. A touch of romance clings to the grim legend like
a tender-petalled flower to a rock. It concerns the impress
of a foot, visible on one of the slabs, and a fair princess
who left it there, many centuries ago. Alone of all
that multitude that fled with Siliwangi, she, the consort of
valiant Poerwakali, his son, escaped the general doom,
through the influence of an Arab priest, who had converted her to the true religion. She could not however
save her husband, whom, before her very eyes, she
saw turned into a stone. But in her faithful heart,
love could not die, though the loved one was dead. The
victor vanquished in his turn by her incomparable
beauty, implored her in vain. She would not be sep-

"A progeny like to the spreading crown of the waringin-tree."

Bamboo bridge near Batu Tulis.

arated from her husband's inanimate shape, and building
herself a little hut under the waringin trees, she still,
day by day, repaired to the stone, which bore Poerwakali's semblance, with sacrifices and prayers and tears.
And often, in a transport of love and grief, she would
throw her arms about the inert mass, closely embracing
it, and, into its deaf ear, murmur soft words and vows

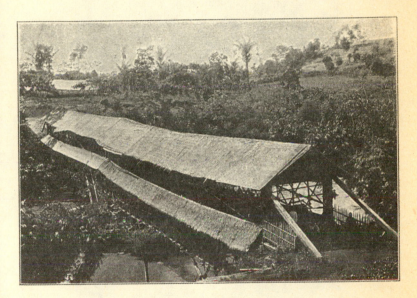

Bamboo-bridge across the Tji-taroon.

of eternal loyalty, and bitter-sweet memories of the
days that were no more. Her tears, still flowing, fell
on the stone underfoot, day by day, month by month,
year by year, until at last it became soft and yielding
as clay, and received and retained the impress of those
tender feet, which for so long had known no other
resting place.

From these memories of an empire overthrown, a

religion smitten with the edge of the sword, and a
love stronger than death—" old unhappy far-off things
and battles long ago"—suggested by Batu Tulis, to
the gaiety of the Buitenzorg races is a wide step. But

Bamboo-bridge across the Tji-taroon.

our modern souls have grown accustomed to these sudden
transitions. In Java, more than in any other country,
one must be prepared at any moment to pass from
the fairy lands forlorn of history, to contemporary
Philistia. Let me hasten to add, in justice, that I found

that high festival of Philistinism in Java, the Buitenzorg races, both amusing and full of interest. The crowded Stands gave one an "impression d'ensemble" of society in the colony, such as would be expected in vain on any other occasion—formal functionaries and business men from the hot towns with their exquisitely dressed, palefaced wives and daughters, mingling with sunburnt planters from the interior, and rosy-cheeked girls from the neighbouring hill-stations, in white muslin frocks, brightened up by flowers such as those grown at home. And the spectacle of the races, exciting in itself, is rendered the more interesting by the changes and transformations which an essentially northern sport has suffered under the sun of the tropics—by the substitution of Sandalwood and Battak-ponies for horses, of native syces, who clutch the stirrup with bare toes, for jockeys, and of silent multitudes brightly garbed, for the black-coated crowds that shout and huzza at Epsom or Longchamps.

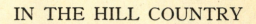

IN THE HILL COUNTRY

Among other Western ideas and institutions, the Hollanders have imported into Java that of health-resorts. Erstwhile lonely hills now bear hotels and „pavilions" upon their disforested summits; picnics are held in glades, where, a few years ago, the timid antelopes fed; and Strauss's waltzes have reduced to silence the noisy cicadas. In the country south and east of Batavia, in the Gedeh-hills, and in the Preanger district, there are several of these hill-stations. There the air is pure and cool, in the months when the hot east monsoon scorches the plains. There is Tji-Panas, Tji-Bodas, Sookaboomi, Sindanglaya, Tjandjoor, the country round about Bandong, and somewhat farther east, Garoot, all of which places are easily accessible from Batavia. The hotels are generally airy, roomy and clean, if not elegant; the food is fairly good, and the charges moderate, about five florins* a day, the average rate throughout Java.

* About 8 to 9 shillings.

The Preanger district, in which Garoot, Bandong and Tjandjoor are situated—the "Garden of Java" as it is fitly named—in more than one respect reminds the traveller of the hillcountry. There is the same clearness in the profiles of the mountain-ranges; the same transparency of the air, which causes distant objects to appear quite near, and reveals their contour rather than their modelling; the same jewel-like sparkle in the colouring of the landscape, in the clear-hued green of valley and hillside, in the changeful hues of the water, and in the blue, opal and roseate violet of the distances under an azure sky. The thin pure air is as wellwater; in the evenings one has to kindle a fire in order to keep warm; and walks of several hours cause neither heat nor fatigue in this bracing climate, which makes even natives quicken their naturally slow movements, and which tinges their brown complexions with a flush of healthy red. In the fields, corn is seen instead of rice, and in places, golden wheat waves. The gardens are fragrant with mignonette, heliotropes, and carnations; mossroses flourish, velvety pansies, geraniums, fuchsias, phlox in all its countless varieties of brilliant colours, and the tender forget-me-nots of northern brooksides. Strawberries, along with clusters of the blue and white grape, show between the dense foliage of the vines. At certain seasons of the year, the hills are purple with the blossoms of the rasamala tree,—a magnificent growth, which throws out its first branches at a height of a hundred feet, and the summit of which reaches an altitude of a hundred and eighty. The most splendid orchids are found in the woods side by side with mushrooms of extraordinary dimensions, some of three feet in diameter, and of strange and brilliant colours. On all sides too, there is sparkle

Girl from Kadoo.

A village couple.

of living water as limpid as the air itself, leaping down the rocky hill-sides in innumerable cataracts and shining in broad tranquil lakes that mirror the encircling hill-tops and the clouds sailing overhead. As one reaches higher levels, from about four thousand feet above the sea-level to six thousand and upwards, the changes in the landscape become more and more marked. The Flame of the Forest, the kambodja, the champaka, and all the countless host of large-flowered trees, characteristic of the tropics, disappear. The type of the foliage changes: it is less fantastic in shape, less luxuriant, and differently tinted from the leafage of the lowland forests. To the sombre green of the plains, which under the glaring sunlight, assumes tones of an almost blackish blue, succeeds a vivid emerald, touched with tender yellow. Then come dense forests of "tjemara" a coniferous tree, the dim greyish foliage of which resembles a drift of autumnal mist; and by and bye, trees of the oak and chestnut-kind appear, and the maple that balances its fan-like leaves on bright red stalks. Violets open their purple chalices in mossy hollows. On the cloudy mountain-heights of Tosari, one may gather flowers such as grow on the Alps. The scenery here is grand beyond description—a landscape of vast hill ranges, cataracts and precipices, and heaving seas of cloud. The temperature is almost too low; big fires are kept burning all day in the hotel, through the verandahs of which the clouds float past. The one thing that still reminds the traveller of the tropics is the wonderful splendour of the orchids that grow here. In the fourth zone, at an altitude of from seven thousand to ten thousand feet, the orchids too, disappear. A European vegetation covers the summits of the mountains and the chill "plateau" of the Djeng, where four wounderful lakes of green, and blue, and yellow, and pure white water sparkle in the sunlight, and the nights are frosty.

These wonders of the Javanese hill-country are well known from the descriptions of many able pens, and from the enthusiastic reports of travellers. But here and there, in the folds of the lower hills, there are pleasant nooks and corners, all but ignored of the multitude, and hardly inferior in beauty to these famous sites, albeit beauty of a very different character. And among these places, the idyllic grace of which has not yet been marred by railroads and hotels, few can surpass in loveliness the country round about Tjerimai, where it was my good fortune to spend several pleasant days, last June.

Tjerimai, a spur of the lofty Preanger range, is situated on the confines of the Preanger Regencies and the Cheribon district, the broad green plains and marshy coast of which its finely shaped summit dominates—a landmark to sailors.

From Batavia, the way thither leads through some of the loveliest scenery in Java—past Buitenzorg and Bandong, straight across the Preanger. Rantja-ekkek, a village in the vast plain, which begins an hour or so east of Bandong, is the last railroad station on the route. There the noise, the hurry and the bustle of western civilization cease, as if arrested by some invisible barrier; and the traveller enters the real Java, the Java of the Javanese, the tranquil land of plenty the inhabitants of which lead their leisurely lives without much more thought of the morrow than the tall gandasoli lilies of their fields. When we two—the friend whom I accompanied to her home among the hills, and myself—reached this stage of our journey, the day was still young. The summits of the hills, which bound the plain on the west, had already assumed their sober day-colours—greyish brown and dark green. But the distant eastern range stood out in violet gleams against a sky of crimson and orange; and the intervening plain was a lake of whitish, waving mist. The air had a peculiar, sweetish taste—like an insipid fruit—which reminded me of early autumn-mornings at home. It was cold, too. Our native servants went with head and shoulders wrapped up: and the breath of the ponies waiting for us at the station made little clouds about their heads. We were grateful for the plaids which we found in the carriage.

The road lay straight before us—a long white streak through the soft misty green of the plain. As we drove along, the pink sheen, which rested on the hazy hillside to our left, like a handful of scattered roses, began to spread and glide down into the valley, kindling as it flowed, until the whole vast vapoury plain was suffused with purple. The mist began to dissolve, and float upwards in little crimson drifts. Suddenly, the great golden sun leaped up from behind the eastern summits, and day streamed in upon us. The country-folk had already begun the labours of the day. Children met us on the road, driving powerful grey buffaloes before them; in a hamlet which we passed, the women were pounding rice, breaking the silence of the morning with the rhytmic click-clack of the wooden pestles. And here and there, groups of labourers moved through the rice fields, weeding. Overhead, larks were soaring and singing; it was the first time I had heard their sweet shrill note in Java. After a while, a partridge flew up with a whirr of hurrying wings, almost from between the hoofs of the horses. They are plentiful in this neighbourhood. At certain seasons of the year, large parties of sportsmen assemble here to shoot them.

On starting from the railway station, I had thought that, in half an hour or so, we should have reached the hill-range, which bounded the plain in the north. But the clear atmosphere has a perspective of its own, confusing to eyes unaccustomed to it. After about two hours of rapid driving we were still in the valley—on either side of us, immense tracts of soft bluish green, full of the thousand lights and shades that form the peculiar beauty of these terraced rice-fields; and all around, the circling summits which seemed no sensibly nearer than at first.

At every turn of the road I expected to reach the base of the hills. And again and again they appeared to recede as we advanced, until the fancy was stirred to the idea of some magic wall environing the captive, withersoever he might turn; and the wish to find an exit out of this hill-bounded plain grew almost to a fever. At length we reached it—a narrow defile between two steep green heights; and the road began to climb. Here, in the deep glens and valleys, the air was notably cooler than on the sunlit plain. Where the road broadened, it was shaded by tall njamploeng trees, which strewed the ground with their white transparent blossoms; and their faint fresh odour, which reminded one of the scent of March-violets, perfumed the breeze.

Meanwhile, we had changed horses at a "gladak"—a nondescript wooden shed—stable, barn and hostelry for native wayfarers in one—with a spacious thoroughfare leading right through it. And our shaggy ponies trotted along with a right good will, until they came to a sudden stand at the bottom of a hill. "Gladakkers," as these ugly litle animals are called, are notorious for freakishness and perversity, and often, without

"A brownie of that enchanted garden that men call Java."

Girl from the Preanger Country.

any apparent reason, will stand stockstill in the middle
of the road, and refuse to move another step. But
this time, as I soon found, they were moved by no
such perverse whim; they knew their duty, and that
the dragging of carriages up this particular hill was in

Javanese of higher class.

no way a part of it. When the syce had unharnessed
them, they turned aside, and began to crop the dewy
grass by the way-side, as if work were over for that
day. And presently, their substitutes, a pair of powerful
grey buffaloes, appeared goaded on by their owner.

Slowly the majestic brutes descended the hill, bending a broad splendidly-horned head and an enormous neck under a triangulor bamboo yoke, and sending forth the breath in clouds from their large nostrils. They drew the carriage up hill without any apparent effort, still moving onward with that same slow, strong, steady gait, which neither the impatient shouts of our syce, nor the goad which their owner plied, could make them accelerate one whit. At the summit they halted of their own accord; and as soon as they felt their necks free of the harness, turned and departed. As they passed me, the curved horn of the one just grazing my shoulder, they seemed to me the personification of resistless strength, unconscious of its own power, and patiently subservient. Their large beautiful eyes had a look of meekness most pathetic in so tremendous a creature.

After this steep hill, the ascent became easy and gradual, and the ponies trotted on at a good round pace. The road still kept zig-zagging between steep hill-sides, densely overgrown with nipah-palm, banana, and dark-leaved brushwood, which shut out the view of the landscape. And I remember no noteworthy incident, except the passing of a native market, a "passar," in a spot where the road broadened a little, and where an impetuous brook, that came bounding down the hillside, spouted from a sort of primitive aqueduct made of bamboo. Half a score of naked children were bathing themselves under the icy "douche," whilst their parents stood bargaining and chaffering at the narrow booths that adhered to the steep hillside like swallows' nests to a house-wall. As we approached, the whole company, men, women and children, squatted down with one accord, as if they had been so many

puppets pulled by a string. One very fat baby, his
fists and his mouth full of sweetmeats, stood staring
at us in round-eyed surprise; but his mother managed
to catch him and draw him to his little haunches, just
in the nick of time; and the whole company remained

Women pounding rice.

in this crouching posture until our carriage rounded
the bend of the road.

At Batavia, where the manners of the natives have
suffered a change—a change for the worse, as some
maintain—by contact with Europeans, I had never witnessed this peculiar mode of salutation. And I confess
I was painfully impressed by it, the more so as my
friend warned me that native etiquette forbade my

acknowledging the humble greeting by so much as a nod. I do not know whether it was the abjectness of their semi-prostration, or the seemingly gratuitous insolence of our thus ignoring it, that I felt as the more acute humiliation to human dignity. But after all, the only way to rightly judge the manners and customs of a country is to look at them from the point of view

The rapids of the Tjitaroon.

of the natives; and to a Javanese, there is nothing undignified in a salutation which impresses us as slavish. He squats down, just as a European rises, in the presence of a superior. It is a token of respect; nothing more. And the superior's apparent unconsciousness of this greeting no more implies rudeness on his part than the familiar nod with which in Europe a gentleman might answer a labourer's or artisan's raising of his cap. "The

Pangeran Adipati Mangkoe Boemi (Djokjakarta).

Javanese Lady.

way of the land, the honour of the land," as the Dutch
proverb puts it.

On the point of etiquette, the Javanese, moreover,
are infinitely more punctilious than any western people
of our period. I believe they might even be said to
surpass the Spaniards of the time of Philip II, in the
elaborateness of their code of manners and in their
strict adherence to its requirements. Every possibl
circumstance and occurrence in life have been foreseen,

Waterfalls.

and the appropriate conduct noted down in the un-
written law of the "adat"; the attitude, the gesture,
and the set phrase, are alle prescribed, down to the
smallest detail. Nor is it a question of phraseology
only; the very language is subject to the regulations
of the adat, which distinguishes three separate and
altogether different kinds of Javanese, according as a
man speaks to his superior, his equal, or his inferior.
For speech to one higher in rank, there is the "Kromo";
commands to a subordinate are given in "Ngoko";

friends familiarly converse in a third idiom into which elements of the other two enter. The theory of these three kinds of Javanese is a science by itself, and one not easily acquired by a westerner. At the same time, it is imperatively necessary to him, if he would gain the esteem of the natives; for the use of a Ngoko word when a Kromo term should have been employed, would mark the offender with an indelible brand of vulgarity and ill-breeding. When the Bible was being translated into Javanese, this peculiarity of etiquette proved a considerable difficulty; and the missionaries had to consult countless authorities and compare a thousand precedents, before they could settle the question whether Christ should address Pilate in Kromo or in Ngoko, or in the third idiom. A solecism would have fatally injured the "prestige" of the new religion: and its ministers could not have escaped the accusation of being "koerang adjar", which being translated into English means "ill-bred." It was in order to avoid this qualification, that my friend and I seeing the country folk at the "passar" squat down in the dusty road, passed on, without so much as looking at them.

Towards eleven o'clock, we reached the highest point of our journey—a ledge upon the mountain-side called Njadas Pangeran. Here the hill on our right suddenly fell away, and the broad green plains of Cheribon lay disclosed, dazzling with sunlight and living water. At our feet, away far below, lay a brown hamlet in the midst of sawahs, like a lark's nest in a field of clover; and the hills, through which we had threaded our way since dawn, hung in the western distance like massy clouds, tinted with brown and violet, and an exquisite, pale, half-transparent blue. We paused here for some minutes, to rest the horses, whilst we gathered armsful

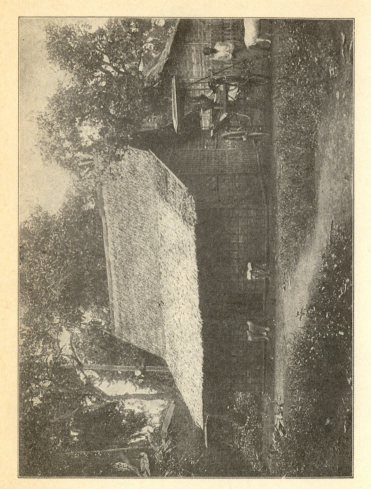

A bamboo hut.

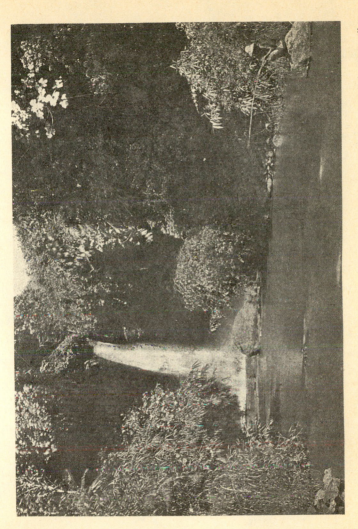

"Through the darkling stillness of the grove there break the splendour and the sound of living water."

of a splendid orchid which grew in profusion on the hillside—great shiny snow-flakes of blossoms, with a touch of carmine on the curling petals; and then resumed the journey along a road which steadily sloped to the bottom of the valley. A muddy river runs through it, which we crossed on a primitive kind of ferry—the carriage, horses, and all standing on a raft, which a score of natives dragged and pushed across the shallow water. On the other bank the road began to ascend again; we had reached the base of Tjerimai, and a drive of some two or three hours more, along a smooth road that passed by prosperous sugar-cane plantations waving in the breeze with thousands of glossy green streamers, brought us at length to our destination—the little bamboo cottage upon the hillside, whither my friends repaired for a spell of coolness and a breath of mountain-air, when the heat rendered the sojourn on their estate in the plains unendurable. It was about four in the afternoon when we entered the garden-gates, and the air was as fresh as in the early morning. The breeze rustled through the tall flower-laden njamploeng-trees on the roadside; there was a smell of water and moist stones in the air; I heard the murmur of a brook over its rocky bed. This was the country of which hot, dust-stifled Batavia was the capital. The thing seemed scarcely credible.

# IN THE DESSA

Our bungalaw on the Tjerimai hillside was situated in the near neighbourhood of a native dessa. But we had been there for some time, before I became aware of the fact. And my first glimpse of the village was a surprise as fascinating as it was sudden.

It chanced in the course of a cool clear morning, as we rode along on our way to the scared grove of Sangean and the legend-haunted lake in its shadow.

We had been skirting for some time, what seemed to be an unusually dense bamboo-wood, when suddenly, in the wall of crowded stems, there appeared a breach and framed in it, lo! a prospect of brown huts, with flowering fruit-trees set between, and a well-kept road in the middle, on which a score of children were playing about. A plough-man came along, driving a pair of grey buffaloes before him, women were coming and going, carrying waterpitchers and piled up baskets of fruit on their erect heads; it was a busy hamlet in the heart of the wood.

We entered, passing from the sunny hillside into the green twilight among the trees, and out again upon the village road, flecked with changeful lights and shadows. It was trim and clean as a gardenpath. The huts on either side of it had a prosperous look,

each standing in its own patch of ground, surrounded
by fruit-trees—mangoes, bananas and djamboos, that
turned the soil purple with their fallen blossoms. The
rice-barns shaped like a child's cradle, narrow at the
base, and broadening out towards the top, were full

Raised shad from which the ripening
fields are watched.

of sweet new rice and in the sheds sleek dun-coloured
cattle stood patiently chewing the cud.

I saw no men about, they were probably at work
on the outlying ricefields. But here and there, under
the pent-roofs of the houses, women sat at their looms
busily weaving sarong-cloth. And on the doorsteps
plump brown babies were rolling about.

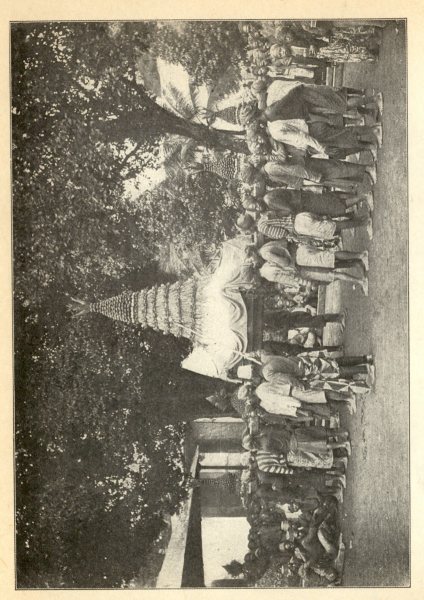

Gunungan, or Pile af Sacrificial Food, as offered by women on Garebeg Mulud, the feast of the nativity of Nabi Muhamed the Great Prophet.

A native official and his followers.

One hut we passed, where a very old man sat playing with a tiny baby, so exceedingly pretty, that we could not help stopping to admire it. With a proud smile he told us, it was his great-grand-child. Its father and mother were living with him, and so indeed were all the other members of his numerous family, sons and daughters and grandsons and granddaughters, who,

Rice-barn shaped like a childs cradle.

each in turn, had wedded and brought a wife or a husband to the parental home.

"There are over a score of them" said the patriarch proudly. To him, in truth, had been granted the prayer, which on their wedding-day Javanese couples put up to the gods. "Give us a progeny like to the spreading crown of the waringin tree." And the venerable sire, trusting in his helpless old age to the love and piety of his children, reminded one of the parent trunk, which, when decaying, is upheld by the stalwart young trees that have sprung up around it.

We asked after his family. The children, the old man answered, were all out in the fields; no hands could be spared from the work just now. Only his youngest grand-daughter, the baby's mother, had stayed in the house, to look after the little one and cook the familydinner. Yonder she was, at her bâtik-frame, painting the sarong-cloth with flowers and butterflies. The girl looked up as he spoke, turning a pretty face on us; and smiled.

"Ah! happy those that live among the woods and fields, if they but knew their happiness..." It seemed to me that these dessa-folk knew theirs.

And I filled my eyes and my heart with the scene before me—the low, brown roofs amidst the fruittrees, the merry-eyed children at play, the leisurely comings and goings of the women upon their daily occupation, with the rustling coolness and the soft green light of the bamboo leafage over it all; gathering all the gladsome beauty of it, that it might keep fresh and fragrant my thoughts, when I should have returned to the world outside, to the weariness, the fever and the fret to which we of the conquering race have condemned ourselves.

As we rode on, and the wood-enshrined hamlet disappeared among the folds of the hillrange, like the beautiful day-dream it all but seemed to me, I learnt that it was but a fair type of the prosperous dessa, such as it is found throughout the length and breadth of Java.

The plan and general appearance of these native villages are always the same — a cluster of huts, each standing in its own patch of ground, surrounded by a quick-set hedge; a main road from which numerous bye-paths diverge, leading through; in the centre an open square, shaded by waringin trees, fronting the mosque : then, surrounding the whole, a dense plantation of bamboo trees, which completely hides the village from sight. Around stretch meadows, ricefields and plantations of nipahpalm, which, in many cases, are the property of the community.

Where this particular form of proprietorship obtains, the village-authorities assign portions of the communal fields in usufruct to such inhabitants of the dessa as will pledge themselves in return to pay certain taxes, and to perform certain duties entailed by the possession of landed property; the principal of which are, keeping the roads and irrigation works in repair, and guarding the gates or patrolling the streets at night. Moreover in all matters touching the cultivation of these fields, they are obliged to observe the prescriptions of the "adat," and such regulations as the village-authorities may deem proper to make.

Very strict supervision is excercised in this matter, so as to prevent the occupant from exhausting, either through ignorance or neglect, the field, which, at the expiration of his lease, will be allotted to another member of the community. Disobedience to the commands of the village-authorities is punishable by forfeiture of the right of occupation.

In most districts, this communal right alternates with private proprietorship.

According to the ancient custom, which has been ratified by the Colonial Regulations, whosoever of his own free will, reclaims a piece of waste ground, by that act acquires the possession of the same, and the right to transmit it to his heirs, the "hereditary individual right," as the legal term is. Any native, desirous to obtain land on these terms, can apply for permission to

Sellers of rice.

the Government, which, having taken the place of the ancient Sultans, is considered as the "Sovereign of the Soil." This permission is never refused. So that, under the communal regime as under the system of heriditary individual ownership, anyone who has the will to work is sure of being able to earn a sufficiency for himself and his family. There need be no unemployed : there are no paupers in our sense of the word. It should be added, that the right of usufruct under the system of communal possession, can be converted into that of "hereditary individual ownership." But the in-

Woman picking cotton, and man plaiting a sieve.

herited communistic sentiment is so strongly developed in the people of the dessa, that they but rarely, if ever, avail themselves of the facilities, which the law offers them in this respect; they prefer that the community should own the soil.

As might be expected, the principle of solidarity, which pervades these laws and customs, manifests itself even more strongly in the domestic life of the dessa-folk.

The ties of kinship—though not those of marriage—
are much respected by them. Parents are so absolutely
sure of the love and filial piety of their children, that

A Javanese family.

they often, as they grow older, abandon all their property
to them, content to live for the remainder of their days
as their sons' and daughters' pensioners. And even the

most distant relation, who, like the nearest, is termed brother or sister, may count in case of need upon assistance and hospitality. Parents are free to bequeath their property as they like; and they sometimes give everything to the first-born son or daughter, without any of the other children protesting. But, just as frequently, the heritage is left to all the descendants in common, when the paternal house is enlarged, so as to

Mat-plaiting.

afford room for all the married sons and daughters and their families; and the produce of the fields is equally divided amongst them, as they equally divide the labour and the toil. Thus, through all chances and changes, the communistic principle is still maintained in the small community of the family, as in the greater one of the dessa. And indeed it may be said that the dessa is but the enlarged paternal house of the Javanese. All the inhabitants of it are his kinsfolk and nearest of blood, whose interests are his own, whose prosperity or misery is bound up with his, and who are his natural allies in defending the common inheritance against the stranger. The bamboo-enclosure which defines and defends the dessa and the environing fields—the common possession of all—are the symbols and the outward visible signs of this.

Such then are the conditions which determine the existence of the Javanese husbandman—a happy life on the whole, exempt from hardship, excessive toil and care, and not without dignity or idyllic grace.

The dessa-man has to work, certainly, but he need not slave; a very moderate exertion is sufficient to procure him what food and raiment he wants. His neighbours are his next of kin, and spite occasional bickerings, his helpful friends. He has himself chosen the village-chief to whose authority he defers, and is free to follow that ancestral law of the adat, which to him is the embodiment of supreme wisdom and justice. And as he goes about his daily business, his labour in wood and field, still keeping time to the recurrent rhythm of the seasons, is graced by many a ceremony and religious rite, which while honouring the gods, rejoices the hearts of the worshippers.

At these religious festivals called "Sedeka," sacrifices of flowers and fruits are offered to the deity and the ancient, naïve idea, that which is pleasant to human beings must also be acceptable to the gods, causes the Javanese to lay on his altar offering of the eatables he is fondest of himself. Such as spice-flavoured rice and all manner of sweetmeats.

In this he does but as Jews and Greeks did before him. But there is a distinguishing detail about Javanese

Women dyeing sarong-cloth.

Weighing rice-sheaves.

sacrifical rites,—a feature, which one is never quite sure whether to call eminently spiritual or naïvely gross and selfish. Of the food offered they believe the deity to enjoy the savour only; the celestial being disdains the

Native official.

material part. And so the worshippers, after a decorous interval of waiting, when they may suppose the invisible and imponderable essence of the meal to have been absorbed by the god, make a cheerful repast on the visible and ponderable parts left on the altar, thus combining piety and high living in one and the same act. In Java, if anywhere, it may be said, that, when the gods are honoured the people fare well.

It would be somewhat invidious to inquire whether piety or appetite be the impelling motive; but from whatever cause, the Javanese are most assiduous in the performance of sacrificial rites. Not only are the cardinal events of human existence, births, marriages and deaths, and the recurrent epochs of the agricultural year honoured with solemn observances, but any and every incident of daily existence is made the occasion of a "Sedĕka."

Sedeka is offered on setting out on a journey, on entering into any contract or agreement, on moving into a new house, on taking possession of a newly-acquired field: the sacrifice being oftenest dedicated to the "Danhjang dessa," tutelary genius of towns and villages; to the spirits who render the soil fertile; to the goddess Sri, protectress of the rice-crops; and to all the ancestors, up to Father Adam and Mother Eve. Then too, side by side with these benignant deities, the wicked "seitans" and djinns are worshipped, the princes of the air, as powerful for evil as Sri and the Danhjang Dessa are for good. It is they who send plagues and pestilence, who make the babe to die at its mother's breast, and the buffalo to drop dead on the half-ploughed field; who cause fires to destroy villages, and floods to sweep away the standing crops; and who seduce men to theft, deceit, robbery, and violence. Since then, they are so powerful for harm, it is wise to keep on terms of amity with them, and give even the Devil his due, bringing him the appointed sacrifices of eggs and yellow boreh-unguent and jessamine blossoms.

These evil spirits, it should be noted, are exceedingly jealous, and one should never glory in the possession of any desirable thing, such as good health, riches, power, or above all, fine children, lest in their spite, they should turn these blessings into curses. But humility, or still better contempt of the things men generally covet, conciliates them. Wherefore a Javanese mother will

Preparing the village field.

often call her child, more particularly if it be remarkable for grace and beauty, by a name implying that it is hateful, ugly and altogether worthless.

Among the saints of El-Islam, Joseph the father of the christian prophet Jesus, is the one whom Javanese matrons venerate above all others; from him they implore the gift of beauty for their children. Nor do they implore in vain. Javanese babies are absolutely charming.

The brilliancy of their black eyes, and the dusky tints of their soft skin give their round little faces a piquancy altogether fascinating. The blue eyes, fair hair and

Native nobleman and his wife.

pale complexion of European children seem insiped by comparison. Now and then one sees faces amongst them, innocent and earnest as those which on Murillo's canvases surround the Madonna in cloud-like clusters.

But alas! these heavenly memories fade soon. The sun of a few East-monsoons utterly wither them. Villon,

Pilgrims returned from Mecca.

could he see the grown-up youths and maidens of Java, would vary his melancholy refrain about fair dead ladies. "But where are the babes of yester-year?"

Among adults beauty is as rare as among children it is common. So that after all it seems Saint Joseph takes the prayer for fine childeren "at the foot of the letter" and answers the petition in a somewhat ironical spirit.

Of the many "Sedeka's" which grace the agricultural year, those connected with the cultivation of the rice-plant are the most important. Java is essentially what, according to tradition, its ancient name betokens—the Land of the Rice. The whole island is one vast rice-field. Rice on the swampy plains, rice on the rising ground, rice on the slopes, rice on the very summits of the hills. From the sod under one's feet to the utter-most verge of the horizon, everything has one and the same colour, the bluish green of the young, or the tawny gold of the ripened rice. The natives are all, without exception, tillers of the soil, who reckon their lives by seasons of planting and reaping, whose happi-ness or misery is synonymous with the abundance or the dearth of the precious grain. And the great national feast is the harvest home, with its crowning ceremony of the Wedding of the Rice.

In order to approximately understand the meaning of this strange rite, it should be borne in mind that a Javanese, similar in this respect to the ancient Greek, believes all nature to be endowed with a semi-divine life. To him a tree is not a mere vegetable, nor a rock a mere mass of stone, nor the sea a mere body of water, any more than he regards a human being as a mere aggregate of flesh, blood, and bone. A hidden principle of life, invisible, imponderable, and powerful for good or evil, animates the seemingly inert matter. In this sense, a Javanese believes in the *soul* of a plant or a rock almost as he believes in the soul of a human being. And this soul he endeavours to propitiate with prayers, libations and offerings of fruit and flowers. Hence the frequent altars under old waringin-trees, in which the Danhjang dessa, tutelary genius of towns and villages, is believed to dwell. Hence the solemn

A scholar.

sacrifices to the Lady of the Sea, Njai Loro Kidoel, who has her shrine on the rocky south-coast. And hence too the rites in honour of Dewi Sri, the Javanese Demeter, whose soul animates the rice-plant,—rites which culminate in the Wedding of the Rice.

At every Harvest-Home this mystical ceremony, the Pari Penganten, is celebrated; and the manner of its conducting is as follows:

As soon as the owner of a field sees his rice ripening, he goes to the "dookoon-sawah" literally, the "medicine man of the rice-field," to consult him as to the day and hour, when it will be meet to begin the harvest. This to a Javanese, is a most important matter, and it requires all the astrological, necromantic and cabalistic knowledge of the dookoon-sawah to settle it. For there are many unlucky days in the Javanese year, and any enterprise begun on such a day is doomed to inevitable failure. After long and intricate calculations, into which the cabalistic values corresponding to the year, the month, the day, and the hour enter, an acceptable date is at last fixed upon by the dookoon-sawah, on which the selection of the Rice-Bride and Bridegroom is to take place.

On the appointed day, having first solemnly consecrated the field by walking round it with a bundle of burning rice-straw in his hand, and by the planting of tall glagahstalks at each of the four corners, invoking Dewi Sri as he does so,—the dookoon begins to search for two stalks of rice exactly equal in length and thickness, and growing near each other. When these are found, four more are hunted for, two pairs of absolutely similar ears of rice. The first couple are the Bride and Bridegroom; the four others the bridesmaids and the "best men," (if the term may be used to designate what the French call garçons d'honneur.) These couples are now tied together as they stand, with strips of palm-leaves, and the dookoon invokes on them the blessing of Dewi Sri. Then he addresses the Rice-Bride and the Rice-Bridegroom, asking

them, each in turn, whether they accept each other
as husband and wife, and answering for them. The
marriage now is concluded; the stalks are smeared
with yellow boreh-unguent, decorated with garlands,
and shaded from the sun by a tiny awning of palm
leaves, whilst the stalks round about are cut off.

Rice-barn.

Now the dookoon, the owner of the field and his
family, all those who have in any way helped in preparing the "Sawah," or planting the rice, sit down to
a "Slamettan," a repast which is at the same time a
sacrifice to the gods, and a further celebration of the
marriage just contracted; and at the end of the banquet,

the dookoon, rising up, solemnly declares that the hour
of the harvest has come.

Now, it is the kindly custom of Javanese land-owners
to invite to the harvest-feast all who, during the past
month, have taken any part however slight in the
cultivation of the Sawah. And as, under so elaborate
a system of agriculture as is demanded by the growing
of rice, these are necessarily many, the Pari Penganten
is a feast for the whole "dessa" as well as for a single

Peasant ploughing.

family. The men leave their work in the shops or the
market, the women lay down the sarong-cloth on which
for weeks and weeks they have been patiently tracing
elaborate patterns with wax, and blue and brown
pigment; and all, in holiday attire and with flowers
wreathed in their hair or stuck into a fold of their
head-kerchief, repair to the ripe rice-field.

The dookoon-sawah is the first to enter it; and as
he does so, he in this wise greets the spirits of the field.

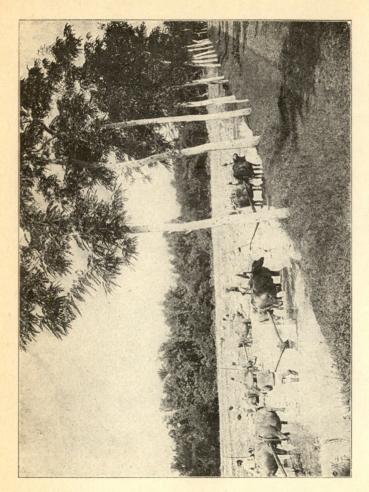

Filling the village field.

Rice on the swampy plains.

"O! thou invisible Pertijan Siluman! do not render vain the labour I have bestowed upon my sawah! If thou dost render it vain, I will hack thy head in two! Mother Sri Penganten! hearken! do thou assemble and call to thee all thy children and grand-children! let them all be present and let not one stay away! I wish to reap the rice. I will reap it with a piece of whetted iron. Be not afraid, tremble not, neither raise

"The produce of the fields is equally divided amongst them as they equally divide the labour and the toil."

thine eyes! All my prayers implore thy favour and gracious protection. Also I propose to prepare a sacrificial repast, and dedicate it to the spirits that protect this my sawah; and to the spirits that protect the four villages nearest to this our village, and also to Leh-Saluke and Leh-Mukalana!"

Having pronounced this invocation, he cuts off the ears which represent the Rice-Bride and Bridegroom

and their four companions, and the reapers begin their
work. The implement they use is best described as a
cross-hilted dagger of bamboo, having a little knife
inserted into the wooden blade; the reaper, holding
the hilt in the fingers of his right hand, with the
thumb presses the rice-stalk against the small knife,
severing the ear, which he gathers in his left hand;
and thus he cuts off each ripe ear separately with a
gesture as delicate as if he were culling a flower. The
whole rice-harvest of Java is reaped in this manner.

The loss of time may be imagined. The Government
has, again and again, tried to introduce the use of the
sickle and more expeditious methods, but in vain. In
all things, the Javanese love to do as their fathers did
before them; and in this particular matter of the reaping of the rice, their attachment to ancestral customs
is still further strenghthened by a religious sentiment.
The Dewi Sri herself they believe, having assumed the
shape of a gelatik or rice-bird, which broke off the
ripe ears with its bill, taught mortals the manner in
which it pleased her that her good gift of the rice
should be gathered. And accordingly her votaries to
the present day do gather in thus, culling each ear
separately. In their opinion, to use a sickle would be
to show a wanton disrespect to the goddess, and a
contempt of her precious gift, as if it were not worth
gathering in a seemly manner; a sacrilege which the
outraged deity would not fail to avenge by famine and
pestilence. On the other hand, what would they gain
by departing from their ancestors' honoured custom,
and adopting instead the manners of the men from
Holland? "Time," these men respond. But then, that
means nothing to a Javanese. He no more wants to
"gain time" than he wants to "gain" fresh air or

sunlight. It is there; he has it; he will always have it. What absurdity is this talk of "gaining" an assured and ever-present possession?

The idea of time as an equivalent for a certain amount — the greatest possible — of labour performed, is essentially occidental. A Javanese not only does not understand it, but he shrugs his shoulders and smiles at the notion. He does not see what possible relation there can be between a day and what these white men call a day's work. He works, undoubtedly; but he works in a quiet deliberate fashion, for just so long as he thinks pleasant or fit, or when the monsoon threatens, unavoidable; and then he stops; and if the task be not finished, well, it may be finished some future day. There is no cause why any ado should be made about it. Everything in time. And let us remember that haste cometh of the evil.

At last however, the harvest in reaped, and the hour has come for the Rice-Bride and Bridegoom to repair to their new home. The two reapers on whom devolves the honourable duty of conducting them thither, don their very best clothes for the occasion, and daub their faces with yellow boreh-unguent. Then to the strains of the gamelan and followed by all the reapers, men and women in solemn procession, they carry the garlanded sheaves to the house of the owner of the field. He and his wife meet them in the doorway; and in set phrase, they inform the Rice-Bride and Bridegroom that the house is swept and garnished, and all thing ready for their reception. The procession then wends its way to the granary, where a small space, surrounded by screens and spread with clean new matting, represents the bridal chamber.

The Rice-Bride and Groom and their "maids and

youths of honour" are introduced into this miniature room, the other sheaves are piled up in the loomboong (rice-born) and when the whole harvest is stored, the dookoon-sawah pronounces the prayer to the goddess Sri.

"The men. with the father of the bride at their head, come for the bridegroom, to conduct him to the Mosque."

"Mother Sri Penganten, do thou sleep in this dark granary, and grant us thy protection. It is meet that thou shouldst provide for all thy children and grandchildren."

Then the door of the loomboong is locked; and during forty days none dare unlock it. At the end of that time the honey-moon of the Rice-Bride and Bridegroom is supposed to be over. The owner of the field comes

"With measured steps the two advanced towards each other, and whilst yet at some distance paused."

to the loomboong, unlocks the door, and in set phrase invites the couple to an excursion on the river. "The boat," he says, "lies ready; and the rowers know how to handle the oars." With this comparison the process of husking the grain is designated.

The sheaves are laid in the hollowed-out tree-trunk which serves as a kind of mortar, and the women, bringing down the long wooden pestles in a rhythmic cadence husk the rice. And this is the end of the Pari Penganten.

But, as the proverb has it, "of a wedding comes a

"Humbly kneeling down, the bride proceeded to wash the bridegroom's feet, in token of loving submission."

wedding" and this mystic marriage of the rice invariably proves the prelude to marriages among the young folk of the dessa, who have met and wooed and won one another during the long days of common work and play in the ripe rice-field. During our stay on the Tjeremai hill-side we had occasion to convince ourselves of this. The Pari Penganten was but just over, when we arrived; and already several marriages were being arranged in the dessa, among the number that of the headman's pretty daughter to a good-looking youth, her remote cousin.

As a preliminary the village scholar had been consulted as to the young couple's chances of happiness; and he having declared the cabalistic meaning of their

Bride and bridegroom sitting in state.

united initials to be "a broadly-branching waringin-tree" which is the symbol of health, riches and a numerous progeny, the parents, reassured as to the future of their children, had begun negotiations about the dowry. This, it should be noted, is given by the family of the future husband.

After a great deal of haggling and protesting, they

had at last agreed upon a sum about half-way between
the amount originally offered by the bridegroom's parents

The wedding-guests on their procession through the village.

and that demanded by the father of the bride. In due
course then, the youth had sent the customary presents
of food, clothes, and domestic utensils to the house of

his bride. And now he was busy preparing himself
for the great day. He had had his teeth filed almost
to the gums, and blackened till they shone like lacquer,
so that his enthusiastic mother and sisters compared
his mouth to the ripe pomegranate, in which the black
seeds show through the red flesh. And day by day
he went to the village-priest to recite to him the words
of the marriage-formula, which he did, sitting up to
his chin in the cold water of the tank behind the
mosque, the priest standing over him, Koran in hand.
The bride, on her side, had been living on a diet of
three tea-spoonfuls of rice and a glass of hot water
per diem, so as to lose flesh and—according to Javanese
notions—gain beauty against the happy day; and to
the great satisfaction of her family, she was now so
thin, that they could almost see the flame of the oilwick
shining through her.

Meanwhile the entire population of the dessa was
busy with preparations for the marriage-feast. The
women might be seen all day long under the pent-roof
of the bride's house and in the kitchen, pounding rice,
boiling vegetables, broiling fish, roasting goats' flesh,
and mixing all manner of condiments for the innumerable dishes, which figure at a Javanese repast. And
the young men were chopping wood and carrying water
as if for their livelihood.

At length the wedding-day arrived.

The sun had hardly risen when already the women
of the village were up and stirring, hastening on their
way to the house of the bride, whom they were to
assist at her toilet. This was a most complicated affair,
the girl's hair having to be dressed in a curious and
elaborate fashion, requiring much twisting and coiling
of oil-saturated tresses, interwoven with wreaths of

jessamine blossom, and fixed with large ornamental pins; and a row of little curls must be painted on the forehead with black pigment. Furthermore the face must be carefully whitened with rice-powder, and the shoulders and arms anointed with yellow boreh-urguent. It need hardly be said that it required the whole morning to bring these many and delicate operations to a satisfactory end.

The men, meanwhile, with the father of the bride at their head, had gone to the house of the bridegroom, to conduct him in solemn procession to the mosque, where the priest was to perform the marriage-ceremony between him and the representative of the bride; for, according to Javanese notions, a woman has no business at a wedding—least of all at her own. From the mosque the groom then returned to his own house, where he proceeded to a toilet hardly less elaborate than that of his bride. After a considerable time, he issued forth again, resplendent with boreh-unguent, garlands of jessamine-blossoms and silver ornaments. He mounted a richly caparisoned pony, which his "youth of honour" held ready for him; and at the head of the procession, triumphantly rode his bride's house, where the guests were waiting, my friends and I among the number, to witness the meeting of the newly-wedded pair.

As the bridegroom drew rein in front of the house, the bride supported by two maids of honour, slowly came out of her chamber. With measured steps the two advanced towards each other; and whilst yet at some distance paused. Two small bags of sirih-leaves containing chalk and betel-nuts were handed them; and with a quick movement each threw his at the other's head. The bride's little bag struck the groom full in the face. "It is she that will rule the roost," said one of the women, chuckling. And I fancied I saw a gleam of satisfaction pass over the bride's demure little face, half hidden though it was by the strings of beads and jessamine flowers dependent from her head dress. The next moment however, she had humbly knelt down on the floor. One of the bridesmaids handed her a basin full of water and a towel; and she proceed-

"The men sat down to a repast."

ed to wash her husband's feet, in token of loyalty and loving submission.

When she was done, he took her by the hand, raising her; and led her towards the middle of the apartment, where a piece of matting was spread on the floor. On this she squatted down, holding up a handkerchief; and the bridegroom threw into it some rice, some "peteh"-beans and some money, symbolising the sustenance which he bound himself to afford her. The symbolical ceremonies were then concluded by his sitting down next to her, and putting three spoonfuls of rice, kneaded into little balls, into her mouth, after which he ate himself what was left in the dish. The solemn part of the proceedings being now over, the festivities began.

As a preliminary, the bridal party was to go in solemn procession through the village; and they were marshalled in order before the door.

A curious cortege it was. At the head appeared two

"barongans", the images of a giant and a giantess, carried on the shoulders of men who were hidden in the large framework; then came the gamelan orchestra, bells, drums, kettles, viols and all; next a group of men mounted on hobbyhorses, and beating on the sonorous "angkloeng." * After these came some half dozen women, carrying the bridal insignia—paper birds, bunches of green leaves and paper flowers, and tall fans made of peacocks feathers. A group of priests followed, beating tambourines and chanting a sort of epithalamium. Next came the bride and her maidens in a litter, carried upon the shoulders of four men;

Native policeman.

and immediately after her the bridegroom on horseback followed by a group of musicians. The wedding-guests brought up the rear.

In this order the procession took the road, went round the dessa twice, and finally halted at the house of the bridegroom.

* An instrument composed of a series of graduated bamboo-tubes.

The father appeared in the door, as soon as he heard the music approaching, came out to meet the procession, and advancing towards the litter of the bride, lifted her out of it and carried her into the house, where the bridegroom's relations were seated in a circle to receive her. To these she was now, with great ceremony, introduced as the daughter of the house, whilst she and the bridegroom saluted every member of the assembly in turn, by kneeling down and kissing his or her feet.

The guests were then invited to enter, and the men sat down to a repast, at which the women served them, whilst the bride and bridegroom took their meal together, separately from the rest.

We took advantage of the momentary bustle to slip away unobserved. There was not a soul to be seen on the moonlit village street; the huts were dark and silent, and at the entrance of the village the watchman on duty for the night had left his post vacant.

A din of laughter and buzzing voices pursued us as we descended the hill-path to our bungalow. And all that night, long after the last cricket had ceased his song, we heard the thin clear notes of the gamelan resounding from the heights.

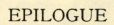

# EPILOGUE

As I write these lines—adding a last touch to the slight sketches in which I have endeavoured to render my impressions of this country—the shrill whistle of steam and the thudding and panting of powerful engines are in my ears, and I see the radiant sky blackened by volumes of smoke. The "campaign" has begun in the Cheribon plains. In endless file the lumbering, buffalo-drawn "pedatis"* creaking under the load of luscious green sugar-cane, jolt along upon the dusty road on their way to the factory yonder,—a great, square, ungainly building, all around which there is a stir and bustle of dark figures, like the swarming of ants around ant-hill. The gate is thrown wide; tall black shapes loom through the semi-darkness of the interior; and now and then the sudden flare from a furnace reveals the bulging, sooty-black mass of a boiler, or the contour of the gigantic wheel slowly revolving. The nauseous smell of the boiling syrup tainst the air.

* Carts the wheels of which are wooden disks.

I went to the mill the other morning, to watch the
transformation of the beautiful tall reeds, which, only
a few hours ago, so gaily fluttered their pennon-like
leaves in the wind and sunshine without, into a shape-
less pulp, and a turbid viscous liquor. The „mandoor"
showed me the first sugar-bags of the season. I looked
at them with some interest beyond that which they
deserved in themselves. We were to be companions
on the journey westwards, and already the steamer
which was to convey us hence, was riding at anchor
in the roadstead of Cheribon.

Last impressions, it is said, are the strongest, and
those whicn ultimately fix the mental images. If so, I
will remember Java, years hence, not as the fairy-land
it seemed to me only yester day, in the sylvan solitudes
of Tjerimai, but as a busy manufacturing country,
prosperous and prosaic.

I will remember a rich soil, an enervating climate,
alternating droughts and inundations and fever-breath-
ing monsoons; a mode of life, comfortable and even
luxurious. but monotonous in the extreme, which taxes
to the utmost both mental and physical energies. I
will think of white dusty towns by yellow muddy
rivers; of hills, and vales, and marshy lowlands overgrown with thick, sprouting rice; of admirable irrigation works; of a system of political administration,
apparently wise and equitable and conducive to the
well-being of a prosperous native population. And I
will be at a loss how to reconcile all these hard solid
facts about Java with the airy fancier, the legends and
the dreams, which must still, as with white splendours
of zodiacal light, illumine my thoughts of the beautiful
island.

It seems impossible that both should be true. And

yet, I know that the fancies are every whit as real and living as the facts, that the poetry and the romance are as faithful representations of things as they are, as the driest prose could be.

Even now, whilst in the factory yonder fires roar, engines pant, and human beings sweat and toil, to change the dew-drenched glory of the fields into a marketable commodity, some hamlet in the plains is celebrating the Wedding of the Rice with many a mystic rite. Some native chief, celebrating the birth of a son, welcomes to his house the "dalang", the itinerant poet and playwright, who on his miniature stage, represents the councils of the gods, and the adventures, in war and love, of unconquerable heroes, and of queens more beautiful than the dawn. And in the sacred grove of Sangean on Tjerimai, the green summit of which dominates the southern horizon, some huntsman, crouching by the shore of the legend-haunted lake, invokes the Princess Golden Orchid and her saintly brother, Radhen Pangloera, who live in a silver palace deep down in the shining water, and who shower wealth, honour, and long life upon the mortal, who pronounces the names the spirits of the lake know them by. Nay— on this very estate, amid the smoke of the factory-chimneys romance still holds her own. The mythopœic fancy of the country-folk has enthroned a "danhjang", tutelary genius of the field, in the branches of an ancient waringin-tree out in the fields. On their way to the mill, men and women pause in its shade, to hang little paper fans on the branches, or deposit on the humble altar jessamine blossoms, yellow "boreh" unguent and new-laid eggs in homage to the agrestic god. Now, the waringin tree stands in a field of sugar-cane, where its wide-spreading roots exhaust the soil, and its broad shadow kills the young plants within an ever expanding circle. Clearly, it should be cut down. But the owner of the estate, warned by recent events, wisely forbears. He chooses to put up with these inconveniences, rather than expose himself and his property to the revenge which the votaries of the Dahnjang would undoubtedly take, if a sacriligious hand were laid on his chosen abode. And so, the Sacred Waringin thrives and flourishes in the midst of the plantations of sugar-cane, a fit symbol of the romance, which, in this island, pervades all things, even those the most prosaic in appearance.

It is this, I believe, this constant intrusion of the poetic, the legendary, the fanciful into the midst of reality, which constitutes the unique charm of Java This is the secret of the unspeakable and irresistible fascination, by which it holds the men of the north, born and bred among the sterner realities of European civilisation. A spell which becomes so potent as to countervail ills, which otherwise would prove unbearable; and to temper, with a regret and a strange sense of want, the joys of the exile's home-coming.

And this too, is the reason why, to me as to so many who have beheld Java not with the bodily eye alone, it must still remain a land of dreams and fancies, the Enchanted Isle where innocent beliefs and gladsome thoughts, such as are the privilege of children and childlike nations, still have their happy home.

# ILLUSTRATIONS

The illustrations marked * are take from originals in the Leyden Ethnographical
Museum, those marked † from the Haarlem Colonial Museum.

Vide also: H. H. Juynboll "Das Javanische Maskenspiel" in: Intern. Archiv
für Ethnographie XIV 41.

L. Serrurier. De Wayang Poerwâ. Eene ethnologische studie, Leiden 1896.

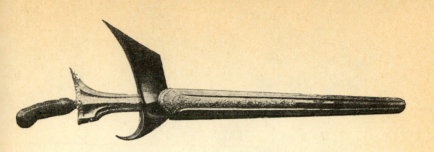

# CONTENTS

**CAMBODIA**
GEORGE COEDES
Angkor

**CENTRAL ASIA**
PETER FLEMING
Bayonets to Lhasa

LADY MACARTNEY
An English Lady in Chinese
Turkestan

ALBERT VON LE COQ
Buried Treasures of Chinese
Turkestan

AITCHEN K. WU
Turkistan Tumult

**CHINA**
All About Shanghai:
A Standard Guide

HAROLD ACTON
Peonies and Ponies

ERNEST BRAMAH
Kai Lung's Golden Hours*

ERNEST BRAMAH
The Wallet of Kai Lung*

ANN BRIDGE
The Ginger Griffin

CARL CROW
Handbook for China

PETER FLEMING
The Siege at Peking

CORRINNE LAMB
The Chinese Festive Board

W. SOMERSET MAUGHAM
On a Chinese Screen*

G. E. MORRISON
An Australian in China

PETER QUENNELL
Superficial Journey Through
Tokyo and Peking

OSBERT SITWELL
Escape with Me! An Oriental
Sketch-book

J. A. TURNER
Kwang Tung or Five Years in
South China

**HONG KONG**
The Hong Kong Guide 1893

**INDONESIA**
S. TAKDIR ALISJAHBANA
Indonesia: Social and Cultural Revolution

DAVID ATTENBOROUGH
Zoo Quest for a Dragon*

VICKI BAUM
A Tale from Bali*

MIGUEL COVARRUBIAS
Island of Bali*

BERYL DE ZOETE AND
WALTER SPIES
Dance and Drama in Bali

AUGUSTA DE WIT
Java: Facts and Fancies

JACQUES DUMARÇAY
Borobudur

JACQUES DUMARÇAY
The Temples of Java

GEOFFREY GORER
Bali and Angkor

JENNIFER LINDSAY
Javanese Gamelan

EDWIN M. LOEB
Sumatra: Its History and People

MOCHTAR LUBIS
Twilight in Djakarta

MADELON H. LULOFS
Coolie*

COLIN McPHEE
A House in Bali*

HICKMAN POWELL
The Last Paradise

E. R. SCIDMORE
Java, Garden of the East

MICHAEL SMITHIES
Yogyakarta: Cultural Heart
of Indonesia

LADISLAO SZEKELY
Tropic Fever: The Adventures of
a Planter in Sumatra

EDWARD C. VAN NESS AND
SHITA PRAWIROHARDJO
Javanese Wayang Kulit

**MALAYSIA**
ABDULLAH ABDUL KADIR
The Hikayat Abdullah

ISABELLA L. BIRD
The Golden Chersonese: Travels
in Malaya in 1879

PIERRE BOULLE
Sacrilege in Malaya

MARGARET BROOKE
RANEE OF SARAWAK
My Life in Sarawak

C. C. BROWN (Editor)
Sejarah Melayu or Malay Annals

K. M. ENDICOTT
An Analysis of Malay Magic

HENRI FAUCONNIER
The Soul of Malaya

W. R. GEDDES
Nine Dayak Nights

JOHN D. GIMLETTE
Malay Poisons and Charm Cures

JOHN D. GIMLETTE AND
H. W. THOMSON
A Dictionary of Malayan Medicine

A. G. GLENISTER
The Birds of the Malay Peninsula,
Singapore and Penang

C. W. HARRISON
Illustrated Guide to the Federated
Malay States (1923)

TOM HARRISSON
World Within: A Borneo Story

DENNIS HOLMAN
Noone of the Ulu

CHARLES HOSE
The Field-Book of a Jungle-Wallah

SYBIL KATHIGASU
No Dram of Mercy

MALCOLM MacDONALD
Borneo People

W. SOMERSET MAUGHAM
Ah King and Other Stories*

W. SOMERSET MAUGHAM
The Casuarina Tree*

MARY McMINNIES
The Flying Fox*

ROBERT PAYNE
The White Rajahs of Sarawak

OWEN RUTTER
The Pirate Wind

ROBERT W. C. SHELFORD
A Naturalist in Borneo

J. T. THOMSON
Glimpses into Life in Malayan Lands

RICHARD WINSTEDT
The Malay Magician

**PHILIPPINES**
AUSTIN COATES
Rizal

**SINGAPORE**
PATRICK ANDERSON
Snake Wine: A Singapore Episode

ROLAND BRADDELL
The Lights of Singapore

R. W. E. HARPER AND
HARRY MILLER
Singapore Mutiny

JANET LIM
Sold for Silver

G. M. REITH
Handbook to Singapore (1907)

J. D. VAUGHAN
The Manners and Customs of the
Chinese of the Straits Settlements

C. E. WURTZBURG
Raffles of the Eastern Isles

**THAILAND**
CARL BOCK
Temples and Elephants

REGINALD CAMPBELL
Teak-Wallah

MALCOLM SMITH
A Physician at the Court of Siam

ERNEST YOUNG
The Kingdom of the Yellow Robe

*\* Titles marked with an asterisk have restricted rights*